DEBATE TO GO

Essential Methods and Practice
for Debating and Discussion

Masakazu Mishima   Jamie G. Sturges

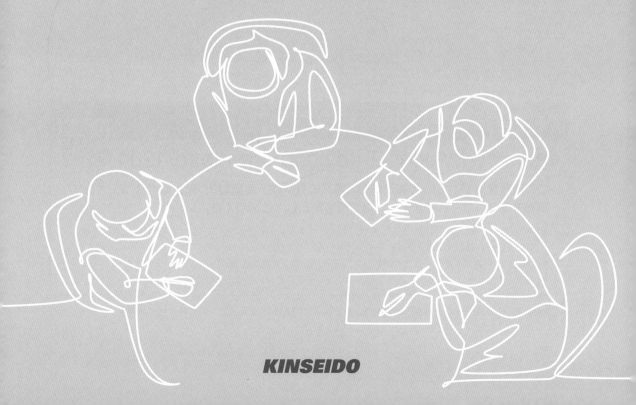

KINSEIDO

First published 2024 by Kinseido Publishing Co., Ltd.

3-21 Kanda Jimbo-cho, Chiyoda-ku,

Tokyo 101-0051, Japan

🎧 音声ファイル無料ダウンロード

https://www.kinsei-do.co.jp/download/4204

この教科書で 🎧 DL 00 の表示がある箇所の音声は、上記 URL または QR コードにて無料でダウンロードできます。自習用音声としてご活用ください。

- ▶ PC からのダウンロードをお勧めします。スマートフォンなどでダウンロードされる場合は、ダウンロード前に「**解凍アプリ**」をインストールしてください。
- ▶ URL は、**検索ボックスではなくアドレスバー (URL 表示覧)** に入力してください。
- ▶ お使いのネットワーク環境によっては、ダウンロードできない場合があります。

◉ CD 00 ▶ 左記の表示がある箇所の音声は、教室用 CD（Class Audio CD）に収録されています。

Preface

Would you like your students to develop the ability to engage in debates in English? *Debate to Go: Essential Methods for Discussion and Debate* is a distinctive textbook designed to aid students in cultivating critical thinking, research, and speaking skills crucial for participating in English debates. This textbook presents carefully streamlined activities that guide students in becoming proficient debaters through active and collaborative learning. Each lesson outlines specific learning objectives along with corresponding activities aimed at constructing knowledge and competencies for conducting debates in either group or pair settings.

This textbook leverages a perspective that transcends the conventional understanding of English language skills and proficiency; it is more than a collection of linguistic knowledge. Rather, it is a participatory and functional competence in social acts involving language use. From this vantage point, debating is perceived as a social act, akin to any other form of communicative interaction. Within the framework of this textbook, the objective is to achieve effective engagement in a debate. The focus shifts towards identifying what needs to be learned by backtracking from the requirements a student must comprehend and accomplish in order to engage in a debate. Consequently, the acquisition of vocabulary, grammar, and other linguistic elements becomes incidental. These components depend entirely on what students recognize as crucial for comprehending the dynamics of a debate, adopting specific roles during the discourse, and effectively fulfilling those roles. This particular approach empowers students to take charge of their own learning journey. Simultaneously, it guides them to seek out any necessary linguistic resources to facilitate debates through collaboration and negotiation.

This textbook caters to English learners at the CEFR B1 (≒ TOEIC score 500) level or above. The content of this textbook intentionally avoids being contingent on students' English language proficiency, as its purpose is to teach the art of conducting debates in a highly accessible manner. Consequently, with appropriate support, it can cater to students with a diverse range of proficiency levels. Furthermore, this textbook has undergone rigorous field-testing over the course of several years within the English program at the Center for Foreign Language Education and Research, Rikkyo University. The outcomes have been exceptionally positive; students have developed the capability to engage in debates in English across a spectrum of topics, irrespective of their proficiency levels.

With this innovative resource, students are not only equipped to engage in English debates but also empowered to shape their own learning journey and confidently navigate the complexities of effective communication.

Masakazu Mishima

Textbook Overview

In each lesson, students can learn and train the following four Skills/Competences:

| 1. Debate Knowledge | Essential knowledge for participating in a debate |

| 2. Speaking | Language expressions useful for effective participation in debates |

	Debate Knowledge	**Speaking**
Lesson 1	• Learn about debate and its structure • Learn about essential terms and phases of a debate	• Show reactions • Check understanding • Ask for explanation and repetition, and paraphrase others and yourself
Lesson 2	• Learn about Propositions • Learn about Constructing Arguments	• Present arguments
Lesson 3	• Learn how to evaluate sources • Learn how to find reliable sources • Learn how to use sources in your debate	• Support your statement with sources
Lesson 4	• Learn about Cross Examination	• Ask questions when cross-examining • Respond to questions when cross-examining
Lesson 5	• Learn about Rebuttal	• Present your counterargument
Lesson 6	• Learn about "Flowing" • Learn about a summary in a debate	• Present a summary
Lesson 7	• Learn about judging a debate • Learn about Debate Performance Assessment Rubric	• Present your debate assessment
Lesson 8-9	• Demonstrate a debate	• Fulfill your role as a debater
Lesson 10	• Review Constructing Arguments	• Present Arguments (Review) • Learn Advanced Expressions for Constructing Arguments
Lesson 11	• Review Cross Examination	• Ask questions when cross-examining (Review) • Respond to questions when cross-examining (Review) • Learn Advanced Expressions for Cross Examination
Lesson 12	• Review Debate Terminologies • Review Rebuttal • Review Summary	• Present counterarguments (Review) • Present a summary (Review)
Lesson 13-14	• Demonstrate a debate	• Fulfill your role as a debater

3. Critical Thinking Activities/Tasks require critical thinking

4. Interpersonal Communication (Collaborative Learning) Activities/Tasks require collaboration

Critical Thinking	Interpersonal Communication (Collaborative Learning)
• Analyze a sample debate	• Work together to learn the essential terms and phases of a debate
• Construct an affirmative/negative argument	• Work together to prepare an argument
• Evaluate sources	• Share your argument supported by a source with your classmates
• Analyze the opposing side of argument	• Practice Cross Examination with classmates
• Identify weaknesses in arguments	• Work together to choose a topic and decide on a proposition for the mid-term debate
• Evaluate debate summaries	• Share your notes with your classmates
• Evaluate a debate	• Work together to review your arguments, counterarguments, and your roles in your team for the mid-term debate
• Debate Reflection/Reaction	• Work together to conduct a debate
• Construct Arguments	• Work together to prepare for the final debate
• Analyze the opposing side of argument	• Work together to prepare for the final debate
• Analyze the opposing side of argument	• Work together to prepare for the final debate
• Debate Reflection/Reaction	• Work together to conduct a debate

CONTENTS

Lesson 1
What is Debate?

Lesson Goals:

☑ Practice Communication Skills: Comprehension, Clarification, and Paraphrasing

☑ Practice sample topics

☑ Learn about debate and its structure

☑ Learn about essential terms and phases of a debate

Warm-up Activity

Talk to a partner. Say as much as you can. Don't worry about grammar or vocabulary!

1. Talk about your hometown and family.

2. Talk about your hobbies and interests.

3. Talk about a place that you want to visit and why.

Discussion Skills

Comprehension

Reactions		Checking Understanding	Remember!
I see. Right. Sure. Okay. Uh-huh. Really?	Yes, I understand. Sorry, I understand. Sorry, I don't follow you.	Do you understand? Do you follow me? Do you see what I mean?	*Reactions* help you show the speaker that you're listening, and to tell them when you don't understand. *Checking Understanding* helps you make sure that others understand you. If a listener doesn't understand, explain your idea again.

Clarification

Listener: Asking for Explanation	Listener: Asking for Repetition	Remember!
Can you explain? What does {X} mean?	Could you repeat that, please? Could you say that again, please?	*Asking for Explanation* helps you tell speakers that more information is needed to make something clearer. *Asking for Repetition* helps you show when you want something to be said again because you didn't hear it clearly or didn't understand.

Paraphrasing

Listener: Paraphrasing Others	Speaker: Paraphrasing Yourself	Remember!
Do you mean...?	I mean...	**Paraphrasing Others** helps you check that you understand other people's ideas.
So, are you saying...?	What I'm saying is...	
So, in other words, ...?	In other words, ...	**Paraphrasing Yourself** helps you explain your ideas so everyone can understand them.

Practice | Analyzing a Discussion

DL 02 · CD 02

1. Listen to the short disucussion below and fill in the blanks. Next, read the script and answer the following questions.

Nami: Is it important to eat breakfast every day? What does everyone think?

Sota: I don't think it's important to eat breakfast every single day. [1] _____ _____ ?

Hina: [2] _____ . [3] _____ . ?

Sota: [4] _____ . [5] _____ that there are some days when there is no time to eat breakfast. For example, if I wake up late and have to hurry to class, I don't have time to eat breakfast. [6] _____ ?

Hina: [7] _____ . I live far away from campus, so because of a long train commute, I don't have time to eat breakfast some mornings.

Nami: I'm sorry, but I disagree. I think it's still important to eat breakfast every day.

Iori: I agree with Nami. I read online that eating breakfast every day helps with weight control and metabolism.

Hina: [8] _____ . [9] _____ "metabolism" [10] _____ ?

Iori: Metabolism means how the body turns food into energy.

Hina: [11] _____ , Iori, [12] _____ . [13] _____ ?

Iori: Yes, of course. [14] _____ eating breakfast every day helps with weight control and helps turn food into energy.

Hina: [15] _____ . Thank you.

Sota: [16]_____ eating breakfast can give you energy for the day?

Iori: That's right. I try my best to eat breakfast every day so I have energy for morning classes.

Nami: I completely agree!

Sota: [17]_____, I see what you mean, but it's still difficult to do that every day. I just try to eat quickly between classes.

Hina: I agree with you, Sota. In my opinion, if you can't do breakfast every day, at least try to do an early lunch!

Questions

(1) Does Hina ask for more information?   Yes / No

(2) Does Hina ask to hear something again?   Yes / No

(3) Who repeats their own idea to make it clearer? (2 people) Nami / Sota / Hina / Iori

(4) Who repeats someone else's idea to check their own understanding? (1 person)

Nami / Sota / Hina / Iori

2. Discuss the following topics. Use Communication Skills to help your partner(s) understand your ideas and show you understand theirs.

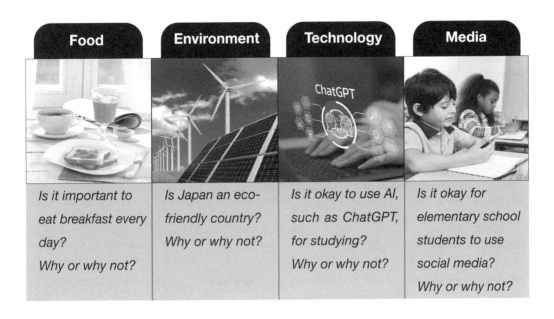

Food	Environment	Technology	Media
Is it important to eat breakfast every day? Why or why not?	Is Japan an eco-friendly country? Why or why not?	Is it okay to use AI, such as ChatGPT, for studying? Why or why not?	Is it okay for elementary school students to use social media? Why or why not?

What is Debate?

1. Think about what you know about debate. Make a list of things you know about debate using the worksheet on Page 91. Share it with your classmates.

2. Read the definition of debate below, and prepare to explain what each of the underlined words mean.

Debate Definition

A debate is a <u>timed and structured</u> academic speaking activity where <u>two opposing teams</u> make speeches to <u>make an argument</u> about a <u>controversial</u> topic.

How is Debate Organized?

A full debate in this class follows the structure below.

	Affirmative Team (AT)	Negative Team (NT)
Affirmative Speech (AS) 5 min	*The AT constructs their arguments.*	*The NT listens to the AS and takes notes.*
Cross Examination (CE) Prep 3 min	*The AT predicts the NT's questions and prepare answers.*	*NT prepares to question.*
Cross Examination (CE) 3 min	*The AT responds to the NT's questions.*	*The NT questions the AT to clarify and better understand the arguments.*
Negative Speech (NS) 5 min	*The AT listens to the NS and takes notes.*	*The NT constructs their arguments.*
Cross Examination (CE) Prep 3 min	*AT prepares to question.*	*The NT predicts the AT's questions and prepare answers.*
Cross Examination (CE) 3 min	*The AT questions the NT to clarify and better understand the arguments.*	*The NT responds to the AT's questions.*
10-minute break for each team to prepare their rebuttals.		
Negative rebuttal (NR) 2 min	*The AT listens and takes notes.*	*The NT rebuts the AT's arguments.*
Affirmative rebuttal (AR) 2 min	*The AT rebuts the NT's arguments.*	*The NT listens and takes notes.*
Negative summary (NS) 2 min	*The AT listens to the summary.*	*The NT summarize all of the arguments from the Negative point of view.*
Affirmative summary (AS) 2 min	*The AT summarizes all of the arguments from the Affirmative point of view.*	*The NT listens to the summary.*

Total: about 40 min

*Each given time may be adjusted if necessary. Follow the time schedule that the instructor gives you.

Debate Terminologies

Debaters need to understand the essential terms and phases of a debate to effectively participate in a debate. In groups or pairs, review the following list of debate terms and ask questions to your peers if you do not understand them.

Term	Definition	Example
Debate Topic (DT)	It is a topic of a debate.	Time management
Proposition	It is a debatable/controversial statement for and against which the two teams will make arguments.	Time management is difficult for university students.
Affirmative Speech (AS)	The affirmative team (AT) makes arguments that agree with the proposition.	We argue that time management can be difficult. For instance, if university students have part-time jobs, they would be too busy to study.
Negative Speech (NS)	The negative team (NT) makes arguments that disagree with the proposition.	Our team believes time management is not difficult for university students because they have had to follow schedules throughout high school.
Cross Examination (CE)	It is to question the other team to clarify and better understand the arguments.	Could you repeat the first reason?
Rebuttal Negative Rebuttal (NR) Affirmative Rebuttal (AR)	After listening to the other team, you respond to their arguments and make arguments against what they said.	Your team said time management was not difficult in high school, but in high school those schedules were often made by our schools, not ourselves. Those schedules also did not include part-time jobs. So, it is not easy to create our own schedules in university.
Summary Negative Summary (NS) Affirmative Summary (AS)	Summarize all of the arguments from your team's view.	Now, I will summarize the debate. We believe it is easy to manage time. While it is true that in high school we followed schedules made by our schools, they still showed us how to effectively manage our time, and we can continue that skill into university, including with part-time work and club and circle activities. Therefore, we are against the proposition.

Listen to the short debate script below and fill in the blanks. Next, read the debate script and identify and highlight the following in the script:

1. Debate topic	**2.** Affirmative Speech
3. Negative Speech	**4.** Cross Examination
5. Rebuttal	**6.** Negative Summary
7. Affirmative Summary	

Maki: Today we are debating the proposition, " [1] _____ _____ ." We strongly believe that living in the city is better than living in the country. It is because there are more job opportunities. [2] _____ , according to a website called "Jojo Kigyo Search," as of April 7th in 2021, Tokyo has 597,717 companies, but Tottori has only 5,170 companies. People in the city have more options. Therefore, we think living in the city is better.

Tatsuya: [3] _____ ? Do you know how many of those companies let workers work from home?

Maki: I'm not sure, but it is well known that many companies allowed [4] _____ _____ from home during the pandemic.

Nao: [5] _____ that living in the city is better than living in the countryside. [6] _____ living in the countryside is cheaper than living in the city. For instance, when I lived in Nagasaki, I paid 35,000 yen for my apartment. However, I'm paying 60,000 yen for the same-sized apartment in Tokyo. [7] _____ , we think living in the country is better.

Shota: [8] _____ the rent you paid in Nagasaki? I couldn't hear that.

Nao: Sure. The rent in Nagasaki was 35,000 yen.

Tatsuya: The other team argued that the city has more job opportunities. [9] _____ , a lot of people work from home now. [10] _____ an online Mainichi news article published on January 30th in 2021, 113 out of the 114 major companies in Japan said they wanted to continue working from home even after the pandemic ends. Therefore, people in the country can also find good jobs.

Shota: [11]_____ that living in the countryside is cheaper than living in the city. It may be true that rent is usually cheaper in the countryside. However, people usually get paid more in the city. For example, according to the Ministry of Health, Labor and Welfare, as of 2021, the minimum wage in Tokyo is 1013 yen while the minimum wage in Nagasaki is 793 yen. Therefore, university students in the city may pay more rent, but they usually earn more money.

Nao: [12]_____. We think that living in the country is better than living in the city because it is cheaper in the countryside. The other team said there are more jobs in the city, but people can work from home in the countryside. Therefore, [13]_____ living in the country is better.

Maki: In conclusion, we are for the proposition. Please remember that there are more companies in the city and this helps people choose a job they like. The other team argued that living in the countryside is cheaper, but people in the city tend to earn more. [14]_____, we think living in the city is better than the countryside.

See Appendix C (Page 66) for a full sample debate.

Homework

1. Review "How is a Debate Organized?"

2. Review "Debate Terminologies"

Lesson 2
Food I

Lesson Goals:

☑ Review debate structure & terminologies

☑ Learn about Understanding Propositions

☑ Learn about Constructing Arguments

Warm-up Activity

Work in pairs:

1. One student reads out any definition in the "Definition" column in the table "Debate Terminologies" on Page 5. The other student says the matching terminology in the "Term" column without looking at the table.

2. Switch roles and do the same.

3. Continue until both students can say the names of all terminologies.

Debate Skills

What is a Debate?

● A proposition is a statement about a topic where there can be reasonable agreement /disagreement.

   Example: **Topic:** Energy drinks

   Proposition: Energy drinks should be banned to avoid health risks.

● When you are assigned to the Negative Team or the Affirmative Team, it does not matter whether you really agree or disagree with the proposition. You should try to think of as many arguments as you can to help your team.

● Some common patterns for propositions are:

   [Common Patterns of Propositions]

   X is Y. Is something true or not?   Example: Energy drinks are bad for health.

   X should/shouldn't Y Something should/shouldn't be done. / Something should change.

     Example: The government should ban energy drink sales to children.

     Example: People should drink more energy drinks to stay active.

Practice

1. Evaluate the following propositions. Are they good propositions for a debate? If not, please explain why not.

  a. Japan should ban smoking in all restaurants.

  b. Ikebukuro Station is not busy in the morning.

  c. Primary school children should not be allowed to eat chocolate.

2. Make a proposition based on this information:

With the Olympics, many restaurants in Japan have had to change from being smoking to being non-smoking. In Japan, the government has been reluctant to introduce a law banning smoking in all restaurants and bars. However, there have been smoking bans for many years in several countries. In 1998 it became illegal to smoke in bars and restaurants in California. The UK introduced a smoking ban in 2007. However, some restaurant and bar owners are concerned that if a ban is introduced in Japan, they will lose customers who smoke.

Constructing Arguments

· Strong arguments logically support the opinion (Affirmative or Negative) of your team.

· Strong arguments are clear and detailed.

· Strong arguments are persuasive.

· Strong arguments use evidence.

Components of an Argument

· Argument = Position Statement + Reason + Evidence

· Making an argument is to express your point of view and to support it with evidence.

· A position statement is a brief expression of your position on the proposition.

· A reason explains why you take that position.

· Evidence supports your claim and strengthens your argument.

Position Statement

Reason
e.g., It's because chocolate decreases the risk of heart disease.

Evidence
e.g., According to a study conducted in 2017, consuming a moderate amount of chocolate was found to reduce the risk of heart disease.

Support

Types of evidence

Type A **Common knowledge or general information**

You can use common knowledge or general information that everyone knows.
You do **not** need to **cite** this.

Type B **Personal experience**

You can sometimes use your own personal experience or experiences of people you know.

Type C **Sources**

You can use information based on research from journals, news websites, books, etc. This type of information is usually facts, statistics, or examples. You should **cite/reference** this information when using them for a debate.

Note: Type C is often considered the best type of evidence for debates.

Practice

1. Work with your partner. Look at the following evidence. Would the evidence help to make an argument stronger or weaker? Be prepared to explain why.

   a. In my experience, soda drinks are bad for your teeth.

   b. According to Dr. Frankie Phillips from the British Dietetic Association soda drinks are bad for your teeth because they are very acidic and can damage the enamel protection on your teeth.

   c. My friend drank many soda drinks and had to go to the dentist to get some false teeth. The dentist said, "Soda drinks are bad for your teeth."

2. Look at the excerpts (a and b) from a debate below. Identify **position statements** and **evidence**. Consider which **types of evidence** (A, B, and/or C) are used in the excerpts.

   a. The other team argued that being a vegetarian is healthy, we think that meat is the best source of some vitamins. For example, meat is a very good source of vitamin B12. It might be true that eating vegetables is healthy, but eating meat can actually help with weight loss. You can get enough protein from meat and eat fewer calories than you would with vegetarian options.

   b. The other team said that vegetarians live longer than meat eaters. However, this isn't really true. In 2005 the German Cancer Research Center found that there was no real difference between vegetarians and meat eaters in how long healthy people live. Therefore, there is no reason to become vegetarian. In fact, it's better to stay a meat eater in terms of health.

Mini-Debate: Constructing Arguments

Work in a group of 4. Divide your group into two teams of 2, and have a mini debate. You will only have an Affirmative Speech (2 min) and a Negative Speech (2 min). When preparing arguments, use the evidence from the Evidence List below, and use the expressions from the Useful Expressions for Constructing Arguments below.

Proposition: Vegetarians are healthier than meat eaters.

Preparation

1. Divide your group into affirmative team (agrees with the proposition) / negative team (disagrees with the proposition).

2. With team members, prepare your arguments. **Each team will speak for 2 min.**

3. When you prepare your arguments, use Useful Expressions for Constructing Arguments on Pages 12-13.

4. Take turns presenting your arguments for **2 min** each.

Debate Preparation Sheet

Proposition: Vegetarians are healthier than meat eaters.
Your team's position: Affirmative /   Negative

Your arguments

Evidence List

- According to the American Dietetic Association, appropriately planned vegetarian diets are healthy, nutritionally adequate, and may provide benefits in the prevention and treatment of certain diseases.
- A study conducted by Dr. Tammy Tong of the University of Oxford found that vegetarians had a 20% higher chance of having a stroke than meat eaters.
- There is a study which examined the nutritional status of elderly Japanese people over 100 years old. It showed that those people's diets contained a higher amount of animal protein compared to the average Japanese person's diet.
- The 2007 report from the World Cancer Research Fund recommends limiting the consumption of red meat and to avoid processed meat intake to reduce the risk of cancer.

Useful Expressions for Constructing Arguments

Debate Opening Statement
Hello everyone. Today we are debating the proposition, "…"

Position Statement
We believe… because… / We strongly believe… because… We think… because… We are strongly for/against this proposition.   *Example:* **We strongly believe that smoking** should be banned in restaurants because it is bad for customers' health and makes the food taste bad.

Organizing Statements
We are going to discuss (insert the number of points) points. Our first point is (that)… Our second point is… Our (first) point is (that)… / My (first) argument is (that)…   *Example:* **We are going to discuss three points. Our first point is that** smoking can increase the risks of lung cancer.

Supporting Statement with Common Knowledge
It's well known (that)… As you know… It's common knowledge (that)… Many people think (that)… As it is often said (that), …   *Example:* **It is well known (that)** there are serious health risks with smoking.

Supporting Statement with Data, Experts' opinions, Facts, and/or Examples
For example / For instance, … Another example is… (Source) found… (Source) says/states… (Source) reports that…. According to (source)… The fact is… This is because / A reason for this is… For example / For instance, …   *Example:* Many countries have successfully banned smoking in restaurants. **For example,** the United Kingdom banned smoking in restaurants in 2007. Another example is New Zealand, which banned smoking in restaurants in 2004.

> *Example:* **According to** a study in 2001, vegetarians live between about four to seven years longer than meat eaters.
>
> **Concluding Statement**
>
> Therefore / For this reason… / For (all) these reasons, we think…
>
> Considering…, we are for/against the idea (that)…
>
> Based on what we have presented, we believe… / we agree/disagree with
>
> > *Example:* **For these reasons, we are for the idea that** smoking should be banned in restaurants.

Reflection

Discuss the following questions with a partner:

- What do you think is a good proposition?
- What is important in constructing arguments?
- Did you use Useful Expressions for Constructing Arguments?

Homework

Write one argument related to food. Make sure to use Useful Expressions for Constructing Arguments.

Lesson 3
Food II

Lesson Goals:

☑ Learn how to evaluate sources

☑ Learn how to find reliable sources

☑ Learn how to use sources in your debate

Warm-up Activity

Work with your classmates:

1. Discuss: Do you eat breakfast every day? Why or why not?

2. You wrote one argument related to food as homework. Share your arguments with your partners. Make sure to use Useful Expressions for Constructing Arguments on Pages 12-13.

Debate Skills | Research: Finding and using sources

Why is Researching Important?

Discuss with your classmates:

Which of the following arguments is more convincing – **a** or **b**? Why?

a. Skipping breakfast is bad for health. According to a 2014 medical study, skipping breakfast has been associated with a 27% increased risk of heart disease.

b. Skipping breakfast is bad for health because I heard it from a friend.

🔑 Researching helps you find sources that support your ideas more strongly. Your arguments become more convincing when you use sources because you can support your ideas not only with your personal experience but also with data and experts' viewpoints.

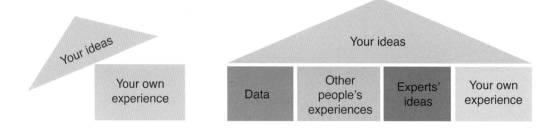

What are Good Sources?

Discuss with your classmates: Are the following sources reliable? Why or why not?

- Online websites
- Research journals
- Data（survey data, statistical data 統計資料, census 国勢調査）
- Newspapers
- Online news articles
- Books
- Blogs
- Magazines
- Wikipedia
- TV shows
- Textbooks

🗝 Researching helps you find sources that support your ideas more strongly. Your arguments become more convincing when you use sources because you can support your ideas not only with your personal experience but also with data and experts' viewpoints.

Evaluating sources

Authors	• Who are the authors? • Is the author an expert on the topic? • What do the authors want to achieve in their writings?
Date	• When was the source published? • Was it written within the past 10 years?
Relevancy	• Is the source relevant to the debate topic & proposition? • Is it important for us?
Data Evidence	• Is the information in the source supported by data? • What types of evidence does the source provide?
Viewpoints	• Does the source discuss a topic from multiple viewpoints?

If one source is not enough to support your argument, you can use multiple sources.

Where do We Find Sources?

Library (university library, city library)

➡ Books, newspapers, magazines, online database

Internet

➡ Identify keywords (e.g., skip breakfast unhealthy) and type them in the search engine (e.g., Google Scholar)

➡ Look at the title and the URL to identify types of the sources (e.g., Wikipedia, news, magazines, blogs etc.)

➡ Check if the source shows the author names and publication dates

➡ Check the first sentence of each paragraph and decide if the source is relevant to your ideas

Recording information about the sources

🔑 Take notes of the following points about the sources. The notes will be helpful when you use the sources in your debate.

Title:

Authors:

Date:

URL:

Key ideas/numbers:

🔑 If you share information about the sources such as authors and a date, you can clearly show where you found the evidence. The opposing team and audience can use the information to judge whether the source is reliable.

🔑 You can check the notes quickly to answer the opposing team's questions when they ask questions about the sources (e.g., When was the online news article published?).

Useful Expressions for Supporting Your Statement with Sources

According to [source – e.g., BBC news], … in [year].

[Source] reports… in [year].

As X argued in [year], …

In their [source] in [year], X discussed…

X wrote a book called [title] in [year]. In the book, the author states (that)…

Example: Our team strongly believes that skipping breakfast is not good for health. **In their** research article **in** 2014, 7 researchers **reported** that men who did not eat breakfast were 27% more likely to have heart disease.

Cahill, L. E. et al., (2014). https://www.ncbi.nlm.nih.gov/pmc/articles/PMC3797523/

Practice | Evaluating sources

Look at the information below and think about the following questions:

1. Can you identify where the information came from?
2. Does the source of the information sound reliable? Why or why not?
3. What additional information about the sources would you like to have?

a. According to a Japanese Ministry of Health, Labor and Welfare report, only 28.7% of young Japanese people have three meals a day.

▶ MHLW, (2014). https://www.mhlw.go.jp/english/wp/wp-hw8/dl/summary.pdf

b. According to a 2014 medical study, skipping breakfast has been associated with a 27% increased risk of heart disease.

▶ Cahill, L. E. et al., (2014). https://www.ncbi.nlm.nih.gov/pmc/articles/PMC3797523/

c. A blogger stopped eating breakfast in 2018 and found that eating breakfast was harmful for their body.   ▶ https://www.xaprb.com/blog/skipping-breakfast/

d. James Gallagher reported in 2016 in an online BBC news article that professor David Rogers at the University of Bristol, UK, points out that children might be missing breakfast because they are from poor backgrounds.   ▶ https://www.bbc.com/news/health-35150598

Practice | Finding sources and supporting your ideas

1. Choose a proposition from the list below and decide your position. Then find a reliable source to support your ideas. Make sure to take notes about the sources.

Proposition 1: Skipping breakfast is good for your health.
Proposition 2: Sushi is healthy food.
Proposition 3: Fast food should be banned at junior high school.
Proposition 4: People should not eat meat every day.
Proposition 5: "Hayaben" (eating lunch before lunch time) should be accepted at high school.

Title:

Authors:

Date:

URL:

Key ideas/numbers:

2. Share your arguments with your classmates using the source. Make sure to use the useful expressions to support your statement with sources. After you finish stating your arguments, discuss the following questions with your partners:

   a. Where did you find the source?
   b. Why did you choose the source?
   c. Are the sources reliable? You can refer to the table "Evaluating Sources" above.

Reflection

Discuss the following questions in pairs or groups:

- Why is researching important?
- What are good sources?
- How can you find good sources?

Homework

1. Find a source about the environment. Read and summarize ideas discussed in the source.
2. Be prepared to share information about the source.

Lesson 4
Environment I

Lesson Goals:

☑ Learn about Cross Examination

☑ Learn how to ask questions when cross-examining

☑ Learn how to respond to questions when cross-examining

Warm-up Activity

In Lesson 3, you were given a homework assignment to find and summarize one source related to the environment. In pairs, talk briefly about the source you found. When you talk, include the following points:

• A short summary of the source   • Why you chose the source

Debate Skills

What is Cross Examination?

● Cross Examination is a phase of debate in which the affirmative and negative teams ask each other questions to better understand their opponents' arguments.

● A good cross examination helps your team find the weaknesses in the other team's arguments.

● To do a good cross examination, you need to be able to ask and respond to questions effectively.

Questioning

When questioning

    What to do: Ask questions for clarification.

    Purpose: To better understand the other team's arguments.

    What to do: Ask questions about data, facts, and/or examples the other team used to support their arguments.

    Purpose: To evaluate the quality of evidence presented to find the weaknesses of the other team's arguments.

Do's and Don'ts

- Do not make arguments; the questioner should ask questions.
- Ask clear and concise questions.

Responding

When responding

What to do: Answer the questions from the other team.

Purpose: To clarify the points raised by the other team.

Do's and Don'ts

- Give specific yet concise answers.
- Do not give too much information. Focus on the question at hand. You do not have to restate all of your arguments and/or evidence.
- Ask for clarification if the question is unclear.

Practice

Listen to the following example of a Cross Examination and fill in the blanks.

A: I have a question. ¹_____, ²_____ that many Japanese car owners wanted to be eco-friendly. ³_____ what you meant when you talked about how many people are buying eco-friendly cars, ⁴_____? Is it still a small number of people?

B: ⁵_____, ⁶_____, a survey ⁷_____ that more drivers are thinking of buying more eco-friendly cars such as hybrid or electric cars.

A: Thank you. ⁸_____. ⁹_____

_____?

B: ¹⁰_____ 2010.

A: ¹¹_____ other surveys since then, and ¹²_____ what they found?

B: ¹³_____, ¹⁴_____. I know that the 2010 survey ¹⁵_____ respected university researchers.

A: Thank you. ¹⁶_____. ¹⁷_____ that *Forbes* magazine found that most customers have a positive image of companies that support environmental issues. ¹⁸_____?

B: ¹⁹_____. ²⁰_____ a very well-respected and well-known business magazine.

Useful Expressions for Cross Examination

Questioning

Asking for Clarification
What was your (first) point? In your first argument you said {summarize}. Could you explain {point that was not clear} please? Does the source say {insert}?
Evaluating the Quality of Evidence
What was the date of {source}? When was {source} published? Is {source} really an expert in this area? How many…?   How much…?
Moving on to the Next Question
Thank you. I'd like to ask another question. Thank you. I have another question. Thank you. I'd like to move on to the next question.

Responding

Giving Clear Answers
Our/My first point was…   It is… Yes.   No. Actually, {explain concisely}. I am sorry, but I don't know.
Responding to Quality of Evidence Questions
The date of {source} was… {Source} was published in… {Source} is {state experience of source}. {Source} has {state experience/qualification}. There are… / There is…
Asking for Clarificationn
Could you repeat the question please? Could you say the question another way? I'm sorry, but I don't really understand the question

1. Use the source you found about the environment and make one argument. You may also use the data, facts, and/or examples below to make an argument. Write your argument in the worksheet on Page 93. When writing your argument, use Useful Expressions for Constructing Arguments in Lesson 2.

Data

- A government survey found that 73% of people were happy to recycle items such as PET bottles, but only 28% of people had tried to buy fewer products.
- According to Business Today, 87% of consumers have a more positive image of a company that supports social or environmental issues.

Facts/Examples

- To try to reduce the number of plastic bags used, many stores in Japan make customers pay money for each bag.
- Long-haul flights produce as much CO_2 as people in some countries produce in one year.

(Example Argument)   DL 05   CD 05

"We strongly believe that the best way to reduce the amount of plastic that people use is to increase the price of plastic shopping bags both in stores and online because it is the only way to stop people buying plastic shopping bags. According to the online newspaper, Japan Today, charging people to pay for plastic bags in shops reduced the number of people buying them by 50% in just two months. However, online sellers of plastic shopping bags reported a 300% increase in sales. This is because the online shopping bags are much cheaper. For this reason, we believe the Government should increase the cost of plastic bags in shops and online."

2. In pairs, practice Cross Examination by following the steps below. Try to use Useful Expressions for Cross Examination as much as possible.

Step 1: Present your argument / Listen carefully and take brief notes
Step 2: Begin Questioning
Step 3: Begin Responding
Step 4: Switch your roles and start over from Step 1.

What Happens before a Cross Examination

Cross-Examining Team Work Flow	Presenting Team Work Flow
Keep notes during the Affirmative/Negative speech	Make Affirmative/Negative speech
⬇	⬇
During 3 minutes Preparation: decide on questions and prepare the question as a team	During 3 minutes Preparation: prepare to respond to possible questions from the other team as a team
⬇	⬇
During 3 minutes Preparation: decide who will ask the questions	During 3 minutes Preparation: decide who will answer the questions
⬇	⬇
Cross Examination (3 minutes)	Cross Examination (3 minutes)

Lesson 4

🔑 Before a Cross Examination, you will have about three minutes to prepare to ask questions to the other team and to prepare for possible questions from the other team.

🔑 To get ready for the Cross Examination, make sure to keep notes during the Affirmative/Negative speech, and decide quickly who will ask what questions/who will respond to questions.

Homework

1. Find one topic that you may be interested in debating. The topic should be related to one of the following categories: Food, Environment, or Technology.

2. Find one source relevant to the topic.

3. Read the source and write a short summary of key evidence you could use for your debate.

Lesson 5
Environment II

Lesson Goals:

☑ Identify weaknesses in arguments

☑ Learn about Rebuttal

☑ Begin to prepare for the Mid-term Debate

Warm-up Activity

Work with your partner. Read the statements below and discuss the potential weaknesses of the arguments.

1. According to research, CO_2 emission is the primary cause of global warming. We argue that we should stop driving cars.

2. Some studies show that a massive earthquake is likely to hit Japan within the next 20 years. Therefore, we should move to the countryside to protect ourselves.

Debate Skills

What is Rebuttal?

● Rebuttal is a phase of debate in which debaters present arguments against the opponents' arguments (counterargument).

● To prepare to rebut, it is important to take notes on the key points that the other team makes during the Affirmative/Negative Speech and Cross Examination.

● To rebut, you need to identify potential weaknesses of the other team's arguments.

● When you are rebutting, consider the following questions:

> **a.** Is the argument the other team gave true? (Accuracy)

Example: "Japan has the tallest mountain in the world."

> (Rebuttal) "**The other team stated** that Japan has the tallest mountain in the world, **but** actually it is Nepal."

> **b.** Does the argument stand up in other cases? (Possible exceptions)

Example: "Japan has four seasons, and because of that it has a large agricultural industry."

> (Rebuttal) "**The other team stated** that Japan has a large agricultural industry because it has four seasons. **That is partially true. However,** Iran is in fact the only country with four complete seasons in the world, and yet its agricultural industry is not as developed as Japan."

> **c.** Does the evidence presented logically support the argument? (Errors in logic)

Example: "Japan is an eco-friendly country because it has many beautiful mountains and forests."

> (Rebuttal) "**It might be true that** Japan has many beautiful mountains and forests, **but** that does not say anything about why Japan is an eco-friendly country."

> **d.** Is the other team's evidence strong enough to support the argument? (Strength of evidence)

Example: "30% of people in Japan do not like fish. To protect the marine environment, we should stop eating fish."

> (Rebuttal) "**The other team argued** that we should stop eating fish because 30% of people in Japan do not like fish, **but** that number is very small. It is only one-third of population in Japan. What about the other 70%?"

The Four-Step Rebuttal

Step 1 Restate

Restate the other team's claim, so that it is clear what you are rebutting. To do this, find weaknesses in the other team's argument. Share your notes with each other and decide what points to rebut.

Example: "**The other team argued** that global warming is a fiction."

Step 2 Rebut

Find a weakness in the other team's claim and make a counter claim. Remember to look for weaknesses in the other team's claim in terms of a) the accuracy, b) possible exceptions, c) errors in logic, and d) strength of evidence.

Example: "**It might be true, but we do not believe that** global warming is a fiction."

Step 3 Give Reasons/Evidence

As a team, develop reasons that support your counter claim. If possible, cite evidence that supports your rebuttal.

Example: "**For example,** if you think of the glaciers melting in the Arctic, the temperature is apparently increasing."

Step 4 Conclude

Summarize your counter claim at the end of the rebuttal, so that it is clear that you have a strong argument.

Example: "**Therefore,** there is no reason to consider global warming is a fiction."

Useful Expressions for Rebuttal

Restate
They/The other team argued (that)…   They/The other team said (that)…   They/The other team talked about…
Rebut
It might be true, but…   It's partially true (that)…   It's not always the case (that)…   The other team said [argument], but [rebuttal]…   However, …   Because…
Give reasons/evidence
For example / For instance,…   Another example is…   [Source] found…   [Source] says/states…   [Source] reports that….   According to [Source]… the fact is…   This is because / A reason for this is…   For example / for instance, …
Conclude
Therefore / For this reason…/ For (all) these reasons, we think that…   Considering…, …

Practice

1. Read the short debate script below. Identify weak claims in the arguments in the script. As a team, use the Four-Step Rebuttal to rebut the weak claim.

> We strongly believe that private car drivers in Tokyo should pay an anti-pollution tax every time they drive into the city center. We think this will reduce pollution and traffic because other major cities have introduced a similar tax. For example, London introduced this kind of tax in 2003 to reduce pollution, reduce traffic, and encourage the use of public transport, like buses.

STEP 1 Restate

Find weaknesses in the other team's claims. Share your notes with each other and choose what points to rebut. Choose your strongest point (the script's weakest point).

Write your restatement of the weak point here:

_____

_____

_____

_____

STEP 2 Rebut

Find weaknesses in the other team's claims. Brainstorm ideas for rebuttals. Think about the a) the accuracy, b) possible exceptions, c) errors in logic, and d) strength of evidence the other team's claims.

Write your counter claim here:

_____

_____

_____

_____

STEP 3 Give Reasons/Evidence

As a team, develop reasons that support your rebuttal. Find and cite evidence that supports your rebuttal.

Write your reasons and evidence here:

_____

_____

_____

_____

STEP 4 Conclude

As a team, write your conclusion for the rebuttal:

_____

_____

_____

_____

2. Put it all together and get ready to present your rebuttal. You can choose one presenter, or each team member can present part of the rebuttal.

Mid-term Debate Preparation

Preparation

Grouping

The instructor will put you into debate groups to prepare for the Mid-term Debates.

Debate Group = All members who are going to have a debate together.

Debate Team = Members in the Affirmative/the Negative Team in a debate group

Debate Topics

The topic should be related to one of the following categories: Food, Environment, or Technology. For any other topics, please consult the instructor.

Step 1 Briefly introduce yourself and exchange your contact information to communicate with each other outside of class.

Step 2 Together in the debate group, choose a topic for the Mid-term Debate. Talk briefly about the topic that you are interested in and present the source you found.

Step 3 Decide on a proposition.

Step 4 Divide your group into the Affirmative Team (agrees with the proposition) / Negative Team (disagrees with the proposition).

Step 5 Together in the debate team, begin searching for sources which can be used to construct your arguments for/against the proposition.

Homework

Develop one argument with evidence from a source. You will share your argument with your team members in Lesson 6.

Lesson 6
Technology I

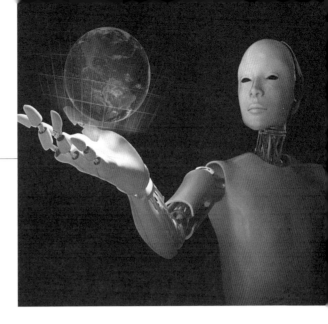

Lesson Goals:

☑ Understand the importance of Taking Notes (Flowing)

☑ Learn about Making Summaries to conclude a debate

☑ Prepare for the Mid-term Debate

Warm-up Activity

Work with a group of three or four students to practice taking brief notes and summarizing information.

1. One student in each group shares what they did in the previous week. Any topic is okay, so please share lots of details!
2. Other students take brief notes about the main things the speaker mentioned.
3. Compare your notes with the others in your group. Did you write the same things? How did you take notes? Did you write down words or did you draw pictures?
4. Repeat so everyone has a chance to be the speaker!

Debate Skills

Taking Notes (Flowing)

- Taking notes, or "flowing," is a very important skill in debates. You need to take notes so that you can make a counterargument or rebuttal against the other team.
- Listen carefully to the other team's arguments. Take clear, brief notes.
- Make notes of the main arguments, evidence, definitions, statistics, and sources.

Making Summaries

What is summary?

- Final stage of the debate
- Comes after both teams have done their rebuttals
- 2-minute summary of entire debate from *your team's point of view*

What belongs in a summary?	What does NOT belong in a summary?

• **Overall summary** of your main points (reasons) from your argument
  ☐ *First, we argued that...*
  ☐ *Second, we argued that...*
• **Focused summary** that restates the rebuttal: which weaknesses did you identify in the other team's argument?
  ☐ *The other team argued that..., but please remember...*
• **Connection to proposition:** restate your team's proposition
  ☐ *For all these reasons, we believe...*
	• New ideas
	  ☐ *We also think...*
	• Additional reasons/examples you did not have time for earlier
	  ☐ *Another reason is...*
	• Questions
	  ☐ *What do you think is...?*

Useful Expressions for Making Summaries

Overall Summary (Give a brief overview)

I'd like to summarize this debate / we told you (about)... because... / we argued (that)... because.... / First, ... / Second, ... / After that, ... / Then, ...

    Example: **First, we argued** (that) technological advancements such as 3D printing could bring many benefits to the world...

Focused Summary (Highlight Key Points)

The first key point was .... / For example, ... / For instance, ... / Another example was ... / The other team argued..., but... / We have talked about... / Please remember (that)... / We said (that)... because... / An important thing to remember is...

    Example: **The other team argued** (that) technology in healthcare has many risks, but **please remember** the risks are quite small and outweighed by the potential benefits.

Connecting Your Summary to the Proposition (Highlight the connection between the summarized points and your position to the proposition)

Therefore, ... / That's why... / As you can see, ... / For (all) these reasons... / ... we support the proposition / ... we are against the proposition / ... we agree with the proposition / ... we disagree with the proposition / That is why you should support the proposition / That is why you should oppose the proposition

    Example: **For all these reasons we support the proposition**, and believe that the government should promote technology in healthcare.

Practice

1. Complete the summary below by adding phrases from the Useful Expressions box. More than one answer is possible.

Proposition: AI (artificial intelligence) will improve healthcare.

Position: Affirmative

Overall summary

1 _____ . 2 _____ reasons why AI will improve healthcare. 3 _____ , we argued that consumers who were surveyed have confidence in AI for healthcare. 4 _____ , we argued that it will be a big boost to the economy. 5 _____ , we argued that it will help the technology and the 3D printing industry grow.

Focused summary

6 _____ that adding AI to healthcare can cost taxpayers a lot of money during a difficult time in the economy, 7 _____ that we believe this cost will be beneficial for the future—our future.

Connection to proposition

8 _____ , we support the proposition that AI will improve healthcare.

2. Review the three summaries below. Which one is a better summary, and why? Use the points in "What is summary?" and the Useful Expressions for Making Summaries phrases to help you.

Proposition: AI (artificial intelligence) is safe.

Position: Negative

A	To sum up this debate, we told you about why AI isn't safe. The first key point was it could be too strong. Next, we said it could be hacked easily. In conclusion, AI isn't safe. Thank you.
B	We'd like to summarize this debate. We told you about the reasons why AI isn't safe. First, we argued that AI could self-improve beyond human understanding. Second, we argued that despite its continuous improvements, AI could still be hacked. The other team argued that AI's safety makes it easier for humans to handle other work responsibilities, but please remember that humans have the added burden of staying aware of AI and its weaknesses. For all these reasons, we do not support the proposition, and believe that AI is not safe.

Lesson 6

C	We'd like to summarize this debate. We told you about the reasons why AI isn't safe. First, we argued that AI could self-improve beyond human understanding. Second, we argued that despite its continuous improvements, AI could still be hacked. We now have another reason. AI could also make it easier for humans to study less. What would happen if we depended on AI too much? AI would learn more but we wouldn't. The other team argued that AI's safety makes it easier for humans to handle other work responsibilities, but please remember that humans have the added burden of staying aware of AI and its weaknesses. For all these reasons, we do not support the proposition, and believe that AI is not safe.

3. Draft a summary of the debate script below for the Affirmative Team (Use the worksheet on Page 95). Remember the points from "What is summary?" and use the phrases from Useful Expressions to help you.

Proposition: AI (artificial intelligence) is safe.
Affirmative Team: Yui, Ran, Aki / **Negative Team:** Moe, Jun, Rei

Affirmative Argument  DL 06 CD 06

Yui: Hello. Today we are here to argue the proposition: AI is safe. We believe that AI is safe. We have two reasons. First, we believe AI can help share the workload of humans. Today, human workers are overworked and, in some countries, like Japan, the number of workers is decreasing. According to a survey in 2023 from Laibo, Inc., found the workers in the IT, marketing, and even construction have used AI chatbots to help them work.

Ran: Our second reason is AI can make lives even safer than they are now. In a 2022 article from Mainichi Shimbun, in Kitakyushu, AI was used to help security in a kindergarten to help detect dangers that could hurt children. This can help parents feel more relief when children are in kindergarten. Therefore, we believe that AI is safe.

Cross Examination DL 07  CD 07

Moe: Yui, you said construction workers use AI. Did the survey say how?
Yui: I'm sorry, but it did not say.
Moe: I have another question. Did the survey say which type of workers used AI chatbots the most?
Yui: Yes, the survey said IT workers used it the most among the workers surveyed.
Moe: Thank you.
Rei: Ran, could you explain how AI is being used in kindergarten?
Ran: Yes, it is being used for security cameras to watch children and warn of danger.
Rei: Thank you. We have no further questions.

Negative Argument

DL 08 CD 08

Jun: Hello. Today we are here to argue the proposition: AI is safe. We are strongly against this position. We have two reasons. First, according to the Future of Life Institute, self-improving AI could move beyond human understanding. The only way around this is for humans to fully understand "all possible modifications", and humans must instinctively know which modifications are safe. But can humans do this? This will only become more and more difficult.

Rei: The second reason is that AI can be used for bad purposes, such as hacking. According to Techopedia, cybercriminals and hackers can use AI to develop more advanced ways to steal people's private information. They can also use AI to pretend to be human users on a social networking site in order to steal information. Therefore, we believe AI is not safe.

Cross Examination

DL 09 CD 09

Yui: Jun, could you explain what "beyond human understanding" means?

Jun: Sure. I think it means to think in ways that people cannot do or ever be able to do. Does that make sense?

Yui: Yes, thank you.

Aki: Rei, you said cybercriminals can use AI on social networking sites to steal people's information. Can you give an example?

Rei: Of course. One example might be fake accounts on Instagram that follow users and send messages.

Aki: I see. Thank you.

Negative Rebuttal

DL 10 CD 10

Moe: The other team argued AI can make lives safer, such as for kindergarteners, teachers, and parents. It's not always the case that AI is being used positively like this, and we believe the dangers of AI being used for bad purposes should have more attention. The fact is for every news article there is about AI being helpful, there are many more that talk about its dangers or cybercriminals using it for stealing private information. This could also happen with that school. Therefore, AI is not safe, in spite of its occasional uses for good.

Affirmative Rebuttal

DL 11 CD 11

Aki: The other team said that AI is dangerous due to hackers stealing private data. That might be true, but businesses are also working hard with AI to keep people safe. Techopedia also explains how businesses, are using AI to build better login safety features and detect fraud. These methods are helping people stay safe, and AI is assisting workers to do this. Considering this reason, AI is safe.

Lesson 6

Yui: We'd like to summarize this debate. We told you about the reasons why AI isn't safe. First, we argued that AI could self-improve beyond human understanding. Second, we argued that despite its continuous improvements, AI could still be hacked. The other team argued that AI's safety makes it easier for humans to handle other work responsibilities, but please remember that humans have the added burden of staying aware of AI and its weaknesses. For all these reasons, we do not support the proposition, and believe that AI is not safe.

Affirmative Summary --

Homework

1. Begin writing a script for the Mid-term Debate and be prepared to perform your role.
2. Review the Debate performance rubric in Appendix B.

Lesson 7
Technology II

Lesson Goals:

☑ Learn about Judging a debate

☑ Be able to judge a debate's strengths and weaknesses

☑ Rate a debate's overall effectiveness

☑ Prepare for the Mid-term Debate

Warm-up Activity

With a partner, discuss a time you were judged. Examples might be a competition, sport, or class activity. Then discuss the questions below.

1. How were you judged?

2. Did you feel you were judged fairly?

3. What is important when judging someone's performance?

Debate Skills

Judging a Debate

● When two teams are debating, you will watch the debate and judge.

● For an evaluated debate, the teacher will also judge.

● The most important judgment to make is to decide which team is more convincing. At the end of debates, audiences usually have a vote for or against the proposition.

● Think about which team had stronger arguments. Were the arguments logical, persuasive, clear, and detailed? Did they present convincing evidence?

● To make a fair judgment, debate judges often use a rubric which describes what to look for in a debate.

Practice

1. Read the following explanation about Debate Performance Assessment Rubric.

How to use Debate Performance Assessment Rubric to judge a debate?

What is Debate Performance Assessment Rubric?

The debate performance assessment rubric is a tool that helps evaluate and assess a debate team's performance based on specific criteria or standards. It provides a clear and organized way to rate how well they have achieved certain goals or objectives. (see Appendix B, Page 64-65). Your instructor will use the rubric to evaluate your team's performance during debate tests.

2. Imagine that you were to judge a debate on the proposition: **"Auto-piloting cars should not be manufactured."** Read **Rubric: Argumentation** and judge the affirmative speech that follows by selecting your response: **c**, **b**, or **c**.

Rubric: Argumentation

Affirmative/Negative Speech should be judged based on the following two categories:

(1) Argumentation (Organization): clear and coherent speech
　説明：議論が論理的に展開されており、明快で一貫性があるかどうか。
　関連する部分：Affirmative/Negative Speech

(2) Argumentation (Quality): Strong arguments: present multiple perspectives and evidence to support them.
　説明：説得力のある議論かどうか、複数の視点から主張が展開されているかどうか、それぞれの視点が根拠を持って提示されているかどうか。
　関連する部分：Affirmative/Negative Speech

Now judge the following speech by choosing **a**, **b**, or **c**.

Affirmative Speech

Mari: We firmly believe that auto-piloting cars should not be manufactured. While the idea of auto-piloting cars may sound appealing, the risks and potential dangers outweigh the benefits. Auto-piloting technology is still in its early stages and has demonstrated numerous flaws. We cannot compromise safety for convenience. Therefore, it is our position that auto-piloting cars should not be manufactured.

Argumentation (Organization)

a. The speech flows logically. Information is organized coherently. (3 points)
b. The speech is generally clear. Information is mostly organized. (2 points)
c. The speech is somewhat unclear. Some incoherent ideas. (1point)

Argumentation (Quality)

a. Present supporting evidence from a wide range of sources. Demonstrates various perspectives.
b. A few arguments are not persuasive due to insufficient supporting evidence. Major issues about the topic are covered.
c. A few potentially persuasive arguments. Most claims are not supported by relevant evidence.

3. Read **Rubric: Cross Examination** and judge the cross examination question and response that follow by choosing your response: **a**, **b**, or **c**.

Rubric: Cross Examination

Cross Examination is judged based on a set of two categories: Question & Response.

(1) Cross Examination Question: Asks clear and specific questions relevant to the argument for clarification and/or asks clear and specific questions related to the quality of evidence.

説明：相手チームに対して具体的かつ明快な問いを行えているかどうか。相手チームの議論に対してさらなる説明を求める質問、あるいは提示された根拠に対する質問を行っているかどうか。

(2) Cross Examination Response: Responds to the questions clearly and concisely. Responds to the questions while not undermining the evidence presented.

説明：相手チームの質問に対し、明快で簡潔に回答しているかどうか。また回答が自チームの提示した根拠と矛盾しないものかどうか。

Now judge the following speech by choosing **a**, **b**, or **c**.

Cross Examination: Question

Kengo: Saki, what measures can we take to address the security concerns associated with auto-piloting technology?

a. The question is specific and clear.
b. The question is somewhat unclear.
c. The question is irrelevant to the argument.

Cross Examination: Response

Takeshi: Mari, don't you think that auto-piloting technology has the potential to reduce human errors and make our roads safer?

Mari: Thank you for the question, Takeshi. While it's true that auto-piloting technology has the potential to reduce human errors, we must acknowledge that it also introduces new risks. The technology is far from perfect and can malfunction, leading to accidents. Additionally, hackers could potentially compromise the auto-piloting system, putting lives at risk. The question we need to ask ourselves is whether the risks outweigh the benefits, and we believe they do.

a. The response is clear and concise.
b. The response is somewhat unclear.
c. The response does not clarify the points raised by the other team.

4. Read **Rubric Rebuttal** and judge the rebuttal that follows by choosing your response: **a**, **b**, or **c**.

Rubric: Rebuttal

Rebuttal: Excellent defense and attack against the opposite side and/or identify major weaknesses of the opposite side. *Demonstrates highly effective team collaboration.

説明：相手チームに議論に対する効果的な反論を行っているかどうか。また相手チームの議論の弱点をついているかどうか。

　　*Debate Test の際は、反論フェーズの前にチーム内での相談の時間が設けられる、このフェーズの準備段階におけるチームの協力度等も評価の対象となる。

(2) Cross Examination Response: Responds to the questions clearly and concisely. Responds to the questions while not undermining the evidence presented.

説明：相手チームの質問に対し、明快で簡潔に回答しているかどうか。また回答が自チームの提示した根拠と矛盾しないものかどうか。

Affirmative Rebuttal

Mari: The negative side argues for the potential benefits, but we must remember that the technology is still in its early stages. Rushing into manufacturing without addressing the safety and security concerns would be dangerous. We should invest in improving existing driving technologies rather than placing full trust in auto-piloting systems that are not yet ready for widespread use.

a. Excellent defense and attack against the opposite side.
b. Acceptable defense and attack against the opposite side.
c. A few successful attacks against the opposite side.

5. Read **Rubric Summary** and judge the summary that follows by choosing your response: **a**, **b**, or **c**. Refer to the points raised in the affirmative speech in Practice 1, if needed.

Rubric: Summary

All key points are clearly and concisely summarized.
説明：自チームの主張が明快かつ簡潔に要約されているかどうか。

Affirmative Summary

Saki: In summary, auto-piloting technology holds great promise for enhancing road safety and accessibility. While concerns about security and flaws exist, we can address them through proper regulations and technological advancements. Let us not deny ourselves the potential benefits by prematurely dismissing this innovation.

a. All key points are clearly and concisely summarized.

b. Some of the key points are summarized.

c. Few or no key points are delivered in the summary.

6. Now listen to the entire debate and take notes about strengths and weaknesses of each team's arguments. Share your notes and discuss:

a. Which team's argument do you agree with and why?

b. What weaknesses are there in the debate?

c. What could help improve the debate?

Proposition: Auto-piloting cars should not be manufactured.

Affirmative Team: Kengo & Mari

Negative Team: Saki & Takeshi

 DL 13   CD 13

Affirmative Speech

Mari: We firmly believe that auto-piloting cars should not be manufactured. While the idea of auto-piloting cars may sound appealing, the risks and potential dangers outweigh the benefits. Auto-piloting technology is still in its early stages and has demonstrated numerous flaws. We cannot compromise safety for convenience. Therefore, it is our position that auto-piloting cars should not be manufactured.

Negative Cross Examination: Question

Takeshi: Mari, don't you think that auto-piloting technology has the potential to reduce human errors and make our roads safer?

Negative Cross Examination: Response

Mari: Thank you for the question, Takeshi. While it's true that auto-piloting technology has the potential to reduce human errors, we must acknowledge that it also introduces new risks. The technology is far from perfect and can malfunction, leading to accidents. Additionally, hackers could potentially compromise the auto-piloting system, putting lives at risk. The question we need to ask ourselves is whether the risks outweigh the benefits, and we believe they do.

Negative Speech

Saki: While the affirmative side raises valid concerns, we should not dismiss the potential benefits of auto-piloting cars. With proper regulations and advancements in technology, auto-piloting can significantly improve road safety. It can minimize human errors caused by fatigue, distraction, or intoxication. Moreover, it has the potential to increase accessibility for people with disabilities. We shouldn't deny ourselves the opportunity to embrace this innovation and its potential benefits.

Kengo: Saki, what measures can we take to address the security concerns associated with auto-piloting technology?

Saki: Thank you for your question, Kengo. Security is indeed an important aspect of auto-piloting technology. To address these concerns, manufacturers can implement strong encryption and authentication systems to protect against hacking attempts. Regular software updates and strict testing procedures can also help identify weaknesses and enhance system security. By focusing on these measures, we can control the risks and ensure a safer experience for all.

Takeshi: While the affirmative side emphasizes the potential risks, we must remember that auto-piloting technology is improving dramatically. Its flaws and weaknesses will soon become a myth. In fact, the risks associated with auto-piloting cars are not so high. Therefore, we should not stop manufacturing vehicles with an auto-piloting function.

Mari: The negative side argues for the potential benefits, but we must remember that the technology is still in its early stages. Rushing into manufacturing without addressing the safety and security concerns would be dangerous. We should invest in improving existing driving technologies rather than placing full trust in auto-piloting systems that are not yet ready for widespread use.

Saki: In summary, auto-piloting technology holds great promise for enhancing road safety and accessibility. While concerns about security and flaws exist, we can address them through proper regulations and technological advancements. Let us not deny ourselves the potential benefits by prematurely dismissing this innovation.

Kengo: In conclusion, the risks associated with auto-piloting cars outweigh the potential benefits. Safety should always be our top priority. Until auto-piloting technology reaches a higher level of reliability and security, we should not manufacture cars with this function. Let's focus on improving current driving technologies rather than rushing into uncharted territory.

Preparation

Get together with your debate team members and do the following:

Step 1 Review the arguments you have prepared with your team.

Step 2 Review what arguments and evidence to present.

Step 3 Practice rebutting potential counterarguments the other team may present.

Step 4 Review the roles in your debate team. Who has what role?

Step 5 Discuss what more is to be done before the debate. Consider the following:
   a. Are your team's arguments strong enough?
   b. Do you need additional resources/evidence to support your arguments?
   c. What Expressions for Debate Skills can you use when performing your role?

Step 6 Practice! With your team, go through the steps of the debate like you would for your mid-term.

Homework

Get ready for the Mid-term Debate.

Lesson 8-9
Mid-term Debate

Lesson Goals:

☑ Complete the Mid-term Debate

☑ Write a debate reflection paper

☑ Write a debate reaction paper

Warm-up Activity

1. Get together with your team members and prepare for the debate (Lesson 8 & 9).

2. Review the rubric and get ready to judge the debates (Lesson 8 & 9).

Debate

● Scheduled debate teams sit front of the class.

● The rest of the students will take notes. The notes will be used to write a reaction paper after the scheduled debates are over.

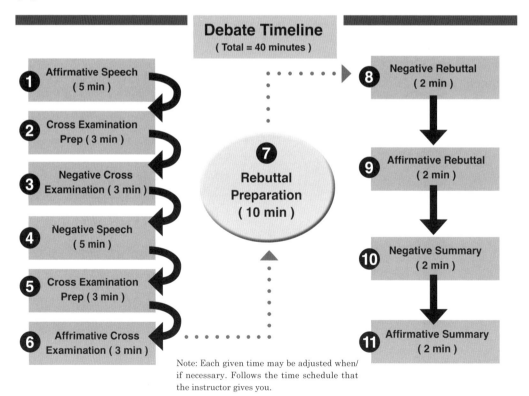

Debate Timeline
(Total = 40 minutes)

1 **Affirmative Speech** (5 min)

2 **Cross Examination Prep** (3 min)

3 **Negative Cross Examination** (3 min)

4 **Negative Speech** (5 min)

5 **Cross Examination Prep** (3 min)

6 **Affirmative Cross Examination** (3 min)

7 **Rebuttal Preparation** (10 min)

8 **Negative Rebuttal** (2 min)

9 **Affirmative Rebuttal** (2 min)

10 **Negative Summary** (2 min)

11 **Affirmative Summary** (2 min)

Note: Each given time may be adjusted when/ if necessary. Follows the time schedule that the instructor gives you.

● In Lesson 8, the teams that had debates become observers in Lesson 9, while the teams that were observers in Lesson 8 will participate in debates in Lesson 9. This way, all members of the class are able to engage in the reflection and reaction of the debates.

●── Debate Reflection ──●

For students who finished the Mid-term Debate.

Discuss the following topics with your team:

- What did your debate team talk about?
- Were you influenced by arguments you heard during the debate?
- How was the debate process?
- How can you improve it for next time?

●── Debate Reaction ──●

For students who observed the debates.

Discuss the following topics with your team:

- Which one of the debates do you think was good and why?
- What did you learn from the arguments you heard during the debates?

Homework

1. Write a reflection or reaction paper (use the forms on Pages 83 and 85).

2. If you judged the debates in Lesson 8 or 9, write a reaction paper about one of the debates. Make sure you include the following points:

- State the proposition
- Explain the arguments made by both teams
- Which team did better? Which team was more convincing? Why?

3. If you finished the Mid-term Debate in Lesson 8 or 9, write a reflection paper about your debate. Make sure you include the following points:

- Things which your team could do better
- Things which you learned from the other team
- How you contributed to preparing for the debate
- What you could do better for a debate next time

Lesson 10
Gender

Lesson Goals:

☑ Review Constructing Arguments

☑ Practice Useful Expressions for Constructing Arguments

☑ Begin to prepare for the Final Debate

Warm-up Activity

Read the information/data below and discuss what you think about the information.

Information/Data

- In 2022, Japan had a wage gap of 22.1% between genders.
- In an online magazine article, *Inc.,* a human capital specialist, Michael Schneider reported in 2018 that more than half of the male workers answered in a survey that they were hesitant to take parental leave because other people might think that they do not want to work. Michael Schneider suggested that companies should not only make a policy but also encourage fathers to take parental leave.
- In a CNN business news article published in 2017, Common Sense Media's parenting editor, Caroline Knorr, reported that TV shows and movies have a long-term influence on how children view gender roles, such as "boys are smarter than girls; certain jobs are best for men and others for women."
- In their research in 2020, Professors Melinda Aley and Lindsay Hahn analyzed 152 popular animated children's films and found that there were more male main characters than female main characters. They also indicated that the male characters in those films were presented as powerful.

Debate Skills | Constructing Arguments Review

Useful Expressions for Constructing Arguments (review)

Debate Opening Statement
Hello everyone. Today we are debating the proposition, "…"
Position Statement
We believe… because… / We strongly believe… because… We think…because… We are strongly for/against this proposition.

Organizing Statements	
We are going to discuss {insert the number of points} points.	
Our first point is…	Our second point is…
Our (first) point is… / My (first) argument is…	

Supporting Statement with Common Knowledge	
It's well known (that)…	As you know, …
It's common knowledge (that)…	Many people think…
As it is often said, …	

Supporting Statement with Data, Experts' opinions, Facts, and/or Examples	
For example, … / For instance, …	Another example is…
{Source} found…	{Source} says/states…
{Source} reports…	According to {source}…
The fact is…	This is because / A reason for this is…

Concluding Statement	
Therefore / For this reason / For these reasons, we think…	
Considering…, we are for/against the idea (that)…	
Based on what we have presented, we believe… / We agree/disagree with…	

Useful Expressions for Constructing Arguments (advanced)

When you report someone's ideas, using different verbs, you can show different nuances.

Neutral	say, report, show, indicate, state
Stronger opinions	argue, believe, support, suggest, emphasize, challenge

Example:
- Caroline Knorr **reported** that TV shows and movies have a long-term influence on how children view gender roles such as "Boys are smarter than girls; certain jobs are best for men and others for women."
- Michael Schneider **suggested** that companies should encourage fathers to take parental leave.

Lesson 10

Read the following propositions and choose one. Then choose your position (affirmative or negative) and construct an argument for the position. If you finish making an argument for your position, make an argument for the opposite position.

Proposition 1: Media is the best way to promote gender equality in Japan.

Proposition 2: Improving a working environment is the best way to promote gender equality in Japan.

• When you support your ideas, you can use your own experiences as well as what you discussed in the Warm-up Activity.

• You can also use the information/data in the Warm-up Activity or you can search for other sources to support your ideas.

• Make sure to use the phrases in the Useful Expressions for Constructing Arguments (review) above.

Advanced: If you can, try to choose an appropriate verb from the Useful Expressions for Constructing Arguments (advanced) on the previous page to show appropriate nuances.

Final Debate Preparation

Preparation

Grouping

The instructor will put you into debate groups to prepare for Final Debates.

Debate Group = All members who are going to have a debate together

Debate Team = Members in the Affirmative/the Negative Team in a debate group

Debate Topics

The topic should be related to one of the following categories: Food, Environment, Technology, Gender or Media. For any other topics, please consult the instructor. Do not choose the topic you have already debated during the mid-term.

Step 1 Briefly introduce yourself and exchange your contact information to communicate with each other outside of class.

Step 2 Together in the debate group, choose a topic for the Final Debate. Talk briefly about the topic that you are interested in and present the source you found.

Step 3 Decide on a proposition.

Step 4 Divide your group into the Affirmative Team (agrees with the proposition) / Negative Team (disagrees with the proposition).

Step 5 Together in the debate team, begin searching for sources which can be used to construct your arguments for/against the proposition.

Homework

Develop one argument on your proposition with evidence from a source. You will share your argument with your team members in Lesson 11.

Lesson 10

Lesson 11
Media I

Lesson Goals:

☑ Review Cross Examination
☑ Prepare for the Final Debate

Warm-up Activity

Work with your partner. You have two minutes to argue two sides of one proposition. When your teacher says "Switch", argue the opposite side of the proposition. Then, your partner summarizes what the speaker said. Switch turns with your partner with the same proposition. Don't worry about grammar or vocabulary!

Proposition: The benefits of social media are bigger than the risks.

Debate Skills Review | Cross Examination Review

Useful Expressions for Cross Examination (review)

Questioning

Asking for Clarification
What was your (first) point?
In your first argument you said [summarize]. Could you explain [point that was not clear] please?
Does the source say [insert]?
Evaluating the Quality of Evidence
What was the date of [source]?
When was [source] published?
Is [source] really an expert in this area?
How many…?
How much…?

Advanced Expressions
Doesn't your evidence show that…
Could your source be biased?
How was the research conducted?
How was the data collected?
You said [summarize], but why…?
Is there any proof (that)…?

Moving on to the Next Question
Thank you. I'd like to ask another question.
Thank you. I have another question.
Thank you. I'd like to move on to the next question.

Responding

Giving Clear Answers	
Our/my first point was…	It is…
Yes.	No. Actually, [explain concisely].
I am sorry, but I don't know.	

Responding to Quality of Evidence Questions	
The date of [source] was…	[Source] was published in…
[Source] is [state experience of source].	[Source] has [state experience/qualification].
There are…/ There is…	

Advanced Expressions
Actually, our evidence shows/doesn't show…
Our source is…
The research was conducted by…
The data was collected by…
The [source] showed…
The reason is…
The source suggests…

Asking for Clarification
Could you repeat the question please?
Could you say the question in another way?
I'm sorry, but I don't understand the question.

Lesson 11

In pairs or groups, each person develops one argument using one of Data/Facts/ Examples below. In turns, present the argument and practice cross-examining using Useful Expressions for Cross Examination (review) on the previous page. In this practice, the person who presents an argument is a respondent, and others are questioners.

Data

- In 2020, over 3.6 billion people around the world used social media and it is expected that approximately 4.41 billion people will be using social media in 2025.
- Young people who use social media for over three hours a day tend to have a higher risk of mental health issues such as low self-esteem and sadness.

Facts/Examples

- Many people use social media to communicate and share photos with friends and family, even if they are in different cities or countries.
- Social media also makes it easy for parents to check what their children are doing and to make sure they are safe.
- Social media can be useful for professional communication. Workers can find new jobs, and companies can find good workers.

Final Debate Preparation

Preparation

Get together with your debate team members and do the following:

Step 1 Share the argument you have prepared with your team.

Step 2 Discuss what arguments and evidence to present.

Step 3 Brainstorm potential arguments the other team may present and discuss how to rebut them.

Step 4 When debating, members of the team are normally assigned a primary role to perform.

Use the list (Debaters' Roles) below and assign a role to each team member. Remember, regardless of your role, you need to work together to prepare for the debate.

Step 5 Discuss what more is to be done before the debate. Consider the following:

    a. Are your team's arguments strong enough?

    b. Do you need additional resources/evidence to support your arguments?

    c. Can you use Expressions for Debate Skills when performing your role? If not, what do you need to do?

Debaters' Roles

Role: Argument Presenters
What to do: Introduce the topic and present the main arguments of your team with specific details. **When to do:** Affirmative/Negative Speech Phase Use Expressions for Constructing Arguments. → see Page 12
Role: Questioners/Respondents
What to do: [Questioners] Listen to the other team's arguments. Try to find points that are unclear and you want more information about. Also, try to find weak points in their argument. Then, ask questions to the other team. / [Respondents] Answer questions from the other team. **When to do:** Cross Examination Phase Use Expressions for Cross Examination. → see Page 21
Role: Counterargument Presenters
What to do: Using your own notes and the notes of your team, present arguments and ask questions to challenge what the other team presented. **When to do:** Rebuttal Phase Use Expressions for Rebuttal. → see Page 26
Role: Summarizers
What to do: Summarize the main arguments. Remember to include both your arguments and any rebuttals. **When to do:** Summary Phase Use Expressions for Making Summaries. → see Page 30

Lesson 11

Homework

1. Begin writing a script for the Final Debate and be prepared to perform your role.

2. Review the Debate performance rubric in Appendix B on Page 64.

Lesson 12
Media II

Lesson Goals:

- ☑ Review Debate Terminologies
- ☑ Review Rebuttal
- ☑ Review Summary
- ☑ Prepare for the Final Debate

Warm-up Activity

Work with a partner. One of you is affirmative, and the other is negative. In one minute, argue your side of the proposition below. Then summarize your partner's argument. Switch roles and repeat. Don't worry about grammar or vocabulary!

Proposition: Playing video games causes violent behavior.

Debate Skills

Debate Terminologies Review

- **Debate** is a formal discussion and type of argument where two opposing teams make speeches to make an argument about a controversial topic.
- **Proposition** is the topic of the debate. It is a statement about something controversial about which the two teams will make arguments.
- **Affirmative Team** makes arguments that agree with the proposition.
- **Affirmative Speech** is the first speech made by the AT.
- **Negative Team** makes arguments that disagree with the proposition.
- **Negative Speech** is the first speech made by the NT.
- **Cross Examination** is to question the other team to clarify and better understand the arguments.
- **Rebuttal:** After listening to the other team, you respond to their arguments and make arguments against what they said.
- **Summary:** Make final arguments and defend against the rebuttals.

Useful Expressions for Rebuttal (review)

Restate
They/The other team argued…
They/The other team said…
They/The other team talked about…

Rebut	
It might be true, but…	It's partially true (that)…
It's not always the case (that)…	The other team said {argument}, but {rebuttal}…
However, …	Because…

Give Reasons/Evidence	
For example / For instance, …	Another example is…
{Source} found…	{Source} says/states…
{Source} reports…	According to {source}…
The fact is…	This is because / A reason for this is…

Conclude
Therefore / For this reason / For (all) these reasons, …
Considering…, …

Practice

Read the argument below and write your rebuttal. Support your ideas with reasons, examples and/or evidence. Present your rebuttal to your partners. Use Useful Expressions for Cross Examination.

Proposition: Media influences kids positively.

Negative Team Speech:

We strongly believe that media has a bad influence on kids. Our first reason is that the media often has some violent scenes. For example, according to a CNN online news article in 2013, 90% of movies, 68% of video games, and 60% of TV programs in the US showed some violence. This may make kids more violent. Another reason is that media can affect kids' health. For example, a website by the Novak Djokovik Foundation reported in 2014 that kids were influenced by idealized body images on TV shows and social media. Some kids try to be too skinny. For these reasons, we think kids are affected by media negatively.

Summary Review

Useful Expressions for Making Summaries (review)

Overall Summary (Give a brief overview)
I'd like to summarize this debate   To sum up this debate, … We told you (about) … because…   We argued… because…   We said… because…   First, … Second, … After that, … Then, …

Focused Summary (Highlight Key Points)
The first key point was ….   Please remember… An important thing to remember is… For example, …   For instance, … Another example was…   The other team argued…, but…   We have talked about…

Connecting Your Summary to the Proposition (Highlight the connection between the summarized points and your position to the proposition)
Therefore, …   In conclusion, …   As you can see, …   That's why… For (all) these reasons ...   … we support the proposition ... we are against the proposition   …we agree with the proposition …we disagree with the proposition   That is why you should support the proposition That is why you should oppose the proposition

Practice

Read the following debate script and write a summary in the worksheet on Page 97. Follow Useful Expressions for Making Summaries on Page 30. Include phrases from the Overall Summary, Focused Summary, and Connecting Your Summary to the Proposition. You may add sample arguments from the Negative Team.

Proposition: Media influences kids positively.

Affirmative Team Speech:

Hello everyone. Today we are debating the proposition "Media influences kids positively." We firmly believe that media influences kids positively. In today's digital age, media plays a significant role in shaping children's lives. We have three reasons.

First, educational programs and interactive platforms provide valuable learning opportunities. Kids can access educational videos, documentaries, and online courses that enhance their knowledge and stimulate their curiosity.

Second, media promotes cultural diversity and fosters acceptance. Through movies, TV shows, and social media, kids are exposed to different cultures, traditions, and perspectives. This exposure helps them develop empathy, tolerance, and a broader worldview.

Third, media can inspire and empower children. Positive role models in movies, TV shows, and books teach important values like kindness, bravery, and resilience. Kids can find characters they relate to and learn valuable life lessons from their stories.

In conclusion, media influences kids positively by providing educational resources, promoting diversity, and offering positive role models. With proper guidance and parental involvement, media can be a powerful tool to educate, inspire, and empower our children. For these reasons, we believe that media influences kids positively.

Final Debate Preparation

Preparation

Get together with your debate team members and do the following:

Step 1 Review the argument you have prepared with your team.

Step 2 Review what arguments and evidence to present.

Step 3 Practice rebutting potential counterarguments the other team may present.

Step 4 Review the roles in your debate team. Who has what role?

Step 5 Discuss what more is to be done before the debate. Consider the following:
   a. Are your team's arguments strong enough?
   b. Do you need additional resources/evidence to support your arguments?
   c. What Expressions for Debate Skills can you use when performing your role?

Step 6 Practice! With your team, go through the steps of the debate like you would for your Final Debate.

Homework

Develop one argument on your proposition with evidence from a source. You will share your argument with your team members in Lesson 11.

Lesson 13-14
Final Debate

Lesson Goals:

☑ Complete the Final Debate

☑ Write a debate reflection paper

☑ Write a debate reaction paper

Warm-up Activity

1. Get together with your team members and prepare for the debate (Lesson 13 & 14).

2. Review the rubric and get ready to judge the debates (Lesson 13 & 14).

Debate

● Scheduled debate teams sit front of the class.

● The rest of the students will take notes. The notes will be used to write a reaction paper after the scheduled debates are over.

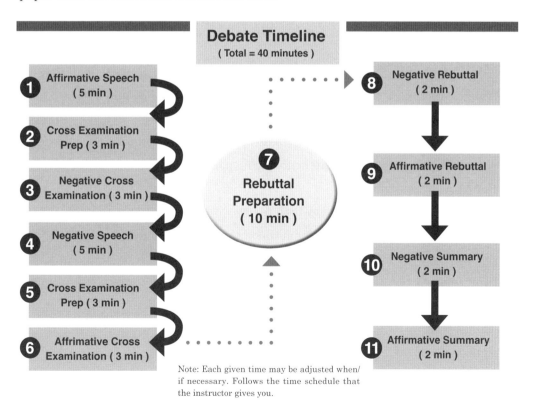

Debate Timeline
(Total = 40 minutes)

1 **Affirmative Speech** (5 min)

2 **Cross Examination Prep** (3 min)

3 **Negative Cross Examination** (3 min)

4 **Negative Speech** (5 min)

5 **Cross Examination Prep** (3 min)

6 **Affrimative Cross Examination** (3 min)

7 **Rebuttal Preparation** (10 min)

8 **Negative Rebuttal** (2 min)

9 **Affirmative Rebuttal** (2 min)

10 **Negative Summary** (2 min)

11 **Affirmative Summary** (2 min)

Note: Each given time may be adjusted when/ if necessary. Follows the time schedule that the instructor gives you.

- In Lesson 13, the teams that had debates become observers in Lesson 14, while the teams that were observers in Lesson 13 will participate in debates in Lesson 14. This way, all members of the class are able to engage in the reflection and reaction of the debates.

• Debate Reflection •

For students who finished the Final Debate.

Discuss the following topics with your team:

- What did your debate team talk about?
- Were you influenced by arguments you heard during the debate?
- How was the debate process?
- How can you improve your debate?

• Debate Reaction •

For students who observed the debates.

Discuss the following topics with your team:

- Which one of the debates do you think was good and why?
- What did you learn from the arguments you heard during the debates?

Homework

1. Write a reflection or reaction paper (use the forms on Pages 87 and 89).

2. If you judged the debates in Lesson 13 or 14, write a reaction paper about one of the debates. Make sure you include the following points:
   - State the proposition
   - Explain the arguments made by both teams
   - Which team did better? Which team was more convincing? Why?

3. If you finished the Final Debate in Lesson 13 or 14, write a reflection paper about your debate. Make sure you include the following points:
   - Things which your team could do better
   - Things which you learned from the other team
   - How you contributed to preparing for the debate
   - What you could improve

APPENDIX

Useful Expressions for Debate Skills

Constructing arguments

Debate Opening Statement
Hello everyone. Today we are debating the proposition, "…"

Position Statement
We believe… because… / We strongly believe… because… We think… because… We are strongly for/against this proposition.

Organizing Statements
We are going to discuss [insert the number of points] points. Our first point is (that)… Our second point is… Our (first) point is (that)… / My (first) argument is (that)…

Supporting Statement with Common Knowledge
It's well known (that)… As you know… It's common knowledge (that)… Many people think (that)… As it is often said (that), …

Supporting Statement with Data, Experts' opinions, Facts, and/or Examples
For example / For instance, … Another example is… [Source] found… [Source] says/states… [Source] reports that…. According to [source]… The fact is… This is because / A reason for this is…

Concluding Statement
Therefore / For this reason… / For (all) these reasons, we think… Considering…, we are for/against the idea (that)… Based on what we have presented, we believe… / we agree/disagree with

Cross Examination Questioning

Asking for Clarification
What was your (first) point? In your first argument you said [summarize]. Could you explain [point that was not clear] please? Does the source say... ?
Evaluating the Quality of Evidence
What was the date of [source]? When was [source] published? Is [source] really an expert in this area? How many…? How much…?
Advanced Expressions
Doesn't your evidence show that… Could your source be biased? How was the research conducted? How was the data collected? You said [summarize], but why…? Is there any proof (that)…?
Moving on to the Next Question
Thank you. I'd like to ask another question. Thank you. I have another question. Thank you. I'd like to move on to the next question.

Cross Examination Responding

Giving Clear Answers
Our/my first point was… It is… Yes. No. Actually, [explain concisely]. I am sorry, but I don't know.
Responding to Quality of Evidence Questions
The date of [source] was… [Source] was published in… [Source] is [state experience of source]. [Source] has [state experience/qualification]. There are… / There is…

Rebuttal

Restate

They/The other team argued…

They/The other team said…

They/The other team talked about…

Rebut

It might be true, but…

It's partially true (that)…

It's not always the case (that)…

The other team said [argument], but [rebuttal]…

However, …   /   Because…

Give Reasons/Evidence

For example / For instance, …

Another example is…

[Source] found…

[Source] says/states…

[Source] reports…

According to [source], …

The fact is…

This is because / A reason for this is…

Conclude

Therefore / For this reason / For (all) these reasons, …

Considering…, …

Making Summaries

Overall Summary (Give a brief overview)
I'd like to summarize this debate To sum up this debate, … We told you (about)… because… We argued… because… We said… because… First, … Second, … After that, … Then, …

Focused Summary (Highlight Key Points)
The first key point was… Please remember… An important thing to remember is… For example, … / For instance, … Another example was … The other team argued…, but… We have talked about...

Connecting Your Summary to the Proposition (Highlight the connection between the summarized points and your position to the proposition)
Therefore, … In conclusion, … As you can see, … That's why… For (all) these reasons… … we support the proposition … we are against the proposition … we agree with the proposition … we disagree with the proposition That is why you should support the proposition That is why you should oppose the proposition

Debate Performance

	3	2
Argumentation (Organization)	✔ The presentation of arguments flows logically. ✔ Information is organized in a coherent manner.	✔ The presentation of arguments is generally clear. ✔ Information is mostly organized.
Argumentation (Quality)	✔ Plenty of strong arguments with supporting evidence from a wide range of sources. ✔ Demonstrates various perspectives, which effectively contributes to the development of arguments.	✔ Many fairly strong arguments but a few are not persuasive due to insufficient supporting evidence. ✔ Major issues about the topic are covered.
Cross Examination*2 Question	✔ Asks clear and specific questions relevant to the arguments for clarification. ✔ Asks clear and specific questions related to the quality of evidence.	✔ Asks questions relevant to the arguments for clarification, but the questions are somewhat unclear. ✔ Asks questions related to the quality of evidence, but the questions are somewhat unclear.
Cross Examination*2 Response	✔ Responds to the questions clearly and concisely. ✔ Responds to the questions while not undermining the evidence presented.	✔ Responds to the questions reasonably well, but the responses are somewhat unclear. ✔ Responds to the questions, but the responses somewhat undermine the quality of the evidence.
Rebuttal	✔ Excellent defense and attack against the opposite side. ✔ Able to identify major weaknesses of the opposite side. ✔ Demonstrates highly effective team collaboration to prepare for a rebuttal.	✔ Acceptable defense and attack against the opposite side. ✔ Able to identify some weaknesses of the opposite side. ✔ Demonstrates effective team collaboration to prepare for a rebuttal.
Summary	✔ All key points are clearly and concisely summarized.	✔ Some of the key points are summarized.

Assessment Rubric

1	0 *1
✔ The presentation of arguments is somewhat unclear. ✔ Some noticeable disorganization of ideas.	✔ No show / No involvement in the debate
✔ A few potentially persuasive arguments. ✔ Most claims are not supported by relevant evidence.	✔ No show / No involvement in the debate
✔ Asks questions irrelevant to some or all of the arguments. ✔ Asks questions fully/partially unrelated to the quality of evidence.	✔ No show / No involvement in the debate
✔ Responds to the questions, but the responses do not really clarify the points raised by the other team. ✔ Responds to the questions, but the responses largely undermine the quality of the evidence.	✔ No show / No involvement in the debate
✔ Fails to defend some issues and/or has few successful attacks against the opposite side. ✔ Minimal team collaboration to prepare for a rebuttal.	✔ No show / No involvement in the debate
✔ Few or no key points are delivered in the summary.	✔ No show / No involvement in the debate

*1 0 should be given to a student who is either absent or does not participate in the debate in any manner. This score category is not team-based and should not be included in the total score for the team. If considered fair, the instructor may give an extra assignment to students who received a 0 to make up for a portion of 15% of the total grade.

*2 The Cross Examination category (i.e., Questioning & Responding together) is worth 3 points.

Sample Debate Script

Introduction -- 🎧 DL 14 ⊙ CD 14

Madoka: Hello everyone. Let me introduce the affirmative team members. My name is Madoka and the other members are Yoshiki and Minami.

Naoya: **Hi everyone.** I'm Naoya and I'm on the negative team with Mayu and Riku. **Today we are debating the proposition**, "Living in the city is better than living in the countryside."

Affirmative Speech (AS) --- 🎧 DL 15 ⊙ CD 15

Yoshiki: **We strongly believe** that living in the city is better than living in the countryside. **We have two main reasons** to support our ideas. **Our first reason is** that living in the city is more convenient than living in the countryside. **It is well known** that there are more shops and restaurants in the city. **For example, according to** a report by Statistics Japan in 2020, Tokyo has 7,391 convenience stores, while some prefectures in the countryside such as Kochi and Wakayama have only 286 and 366 convenience stores respectively.

Minami: **Our second point is** that living in the city gives people more job opportunities. **According to** "Jojo Kigyo Search," **as of** April 7 in 2021, Tokyo has 597,717 companies, Osaka has 237,189, and Kanagawa has 139,720. **In contrast,** some prefectures in the countryside have fewer companies. **For instance,** Tottori has only 5,170 companies. **In addition,** a writer of NBC online news, Mary Pflum, **stated in** 2019 that job opportunities in big cities such as New York and San Francisco would keep growing while some rural areas would be losing jobs. **Therefore,** people have a higher chance of finding a job that they like in the city. **For all these reasons, we think** that living in the city is better than living in the countryside.

Cross Examination (CE) -- 🎧 DL 16 ⊙ CD 16

Mayu: **Can I ask a question? You showed** the number of convenience stores. **Does the website show** the number of convenience stores per population?

Yoshiki: The website **does not have** the information.

Riku: **Can I ask a question? I couldn't understand** the second reason. **Could you repeat** your second reason?

Minami: **Sure. There are** more job opportunities in the city. For example, according to "Jojo Kigyo Search," Tokyo, Osaka, and Kanagawa **have** the greatest number of companies in Japan.

Madoka: **Could you repeat** the data about the number of jobs in Tokyo, Osaka, Kanagawa, and Tottori?

Minami: **Okay.** Tokyo **has** 597,717 companies, Osaka **has** 237,189, and Kanagawa **has** 139,720. Tottori **has** only 5,170 companies.

Madoka: Thank you. **Do you know how many** of those companies allow working from home?

Minami: I'm not sure, but it is well known that many companies allowed remote working from home during the pandemic.

Riku: That's all from our team. Thank you.

Naoya: **We are strongly against the proposition** that living in the city is better than living in the countryside. **This is mainly because** living in the countryside is cheaper than living in the city. **For example, according to** a website by a Japanese real estate company, LIFULL HOME'S, university students in 4 prefectures in the urban area, Tokyo, Kanagawa, Chiba, and Saitama, pay 58,283 yen per month for their rent on average. In Tokyo, the average rent for a one-bedroom apartment is 69,466 yen per month. **On the other hand,** the average rent for the same-sized apartment in the countryside, **for example** Miyagi and Hiroshima, is between 47,000 to 49,000 yen per month. **In addition,** I'm from Aomori and **from my own experience,** I was surprised how expensive vegetables and fruits were in Tokyo when I moved here.

Mayu: **We believe** that living in the countryside is better **also because** it is less stressful. In fact, a psychologist, Juli Fraga, **reported in** 2019 that people in the city tend to experience mental health issues more often than those who live in the countryside. **According to** Juli Fraga, a study **showed** that people in the city have a 21% greater chance of suffering from anxiety disorders as well as a 39% greater chance of experiencing mood disorders than those who live in the countryside. **In conclusion, we believe** that living in the countryside is better than living in the city.

Madoka: **I'd like to ask a question about** the living cost. **You said** the housing and food is more expensive in the city than in the countryside. **Do you know how much** people in those prefectures earn on average**?**

Naoya: **I don't know.**

Yoshiki: **Can I ask another question? Which source did you check when** you learned about Juli Fraga's report**?**

Mayu: **We read** an online website **called** "healthline." **The title of the article is** "Here's how living in the city can mess with your mental health."

Yoshiki: Thank you. **Does the article say** why people in the city are more likely to suffer from those mental health issues**?**

Mayu: **Yes. The author said** that a lot of stimulation in the city area damages the psychological immune system and increases the risks of mental health issues such as depression and anxiety.

Yoshiki: Thank you.

Minami: **Can you explain** what "mood disorders" are**?**

Mayu: Mood disorders **mean** mental or emotional health issues such as depression.

Minami: Thank you. **That's all from us.**

Negative Rebuttal (NR) -- DL 19　CD 19

Riku: **Although the other team said** that there are more convenience stores in the city in Japan, **it does not always mean** that it's more convenient. **As you know,** there are more people in the city area, so people in the city may need to wait as long as those who live in the countryside when they go to shops. **From my experience,** I often need to wait in a long line when I shop at a convenience store in Tokyo, for example, at the convenience store on campus.

Naoya: **The other team also argued** that the city has more job opportunities. **However,** there are now many jobs that allow employees to work from home. **According to** an online Mainichi news article **published on** January 30 in 2021, 90% of the companies, 113 out of the major 114 companies in Japan, **answered** in the survey that they were planning to continue to allow working from home even after the pandemic ends. **Therefore,** more job opportunities **are not necessarily** an advantage of living in the city.

Affirmative Rebuttal (AR) --- DL 20　CD 20

Madoka: **The other team argued** that living in the countryside is cheaper than living in the city. **It may be true** that housing and food costs are usually cheaper in the countryside. **However,** people usually get paid more in the city. **For example, according to** the Ministry of Health, Labor and Welfare, **as of** 2021, the minimum wage in Tokyo is 1,013 yen per hour, while the minimum wage in Miyagi and Hiroshima is 825 yen and 871 yen per hour respectively. **Therefore, although** university students in the city may pay more rent, they usually earn more money.

Yoshiki: **The other team also said** that living in the city causes stress and increases the risks of mental health issues. **The information might be true, but** living in the city can reduce risks of other types of health issues. **For example,** Rachel Nuwer **wrote** in an online BBC article in 2018 that urbanites are less likely to suffer from obesity, and the suicide rate in the city is lower than the countryside. **In addition,** living in the countryside could also cause other types of health issues. **For instance, according to** Rachel Nuwer, 1.1 million citizens in India died in 2015 **because of** air pollution. Seventy five percent of the deaths happened in the rural area where a lot of agricultural fields are burnt.

Negative Summary (NS) --- DL 21　CD 21

Mayu: **I'd like to summarize this debate. We are strongly against the proposition. One reason is** that living in the countryside is cheaper than living in the city. As we said, the rent in the urban area is higher than the countryside. Also, **please remember** that living in the countryside is good for our mental health.

The opponent team argued that living in the city brings some advantages such as more shops and job opportunities. **However,** there is not a big difference between the city and the countryside in terms of the number of convenience stores per population. **In addition, because** more companies have introduced working from home, people in the countryside can also work for a company located in the city area.

For all these reasons, we strongly believe that living in the countryside is better than living in the city.

Affirmative Summary (AS) -- DL 22 CD 22

Riku: **I'd like to summarize this debate. We think** that living in the city is better than the countryside. **Our first point is** that it is more convenient in the city **because** there are more shops. **Our second point is** that there are more career opportunities in the city because there are more companies there.

The other team argued that living in the countryside is cheaper, **but please remember** that people in the city tend to earn more. **In addition, it may be true** that living in the countryside may be better for mental health, **but** people in the city are less likely to suffer from other health issues. **Moreover,** living in the countryside could cause serious health issues **because of** air pollution. **In conclusion, we are for the proposition.**

Debate Skills Glossary with Japanese Explanations

Debate Skills and Terminologies	日本語訳	説明
Debate Topic (DT)	話題（トピック）	ディベートの話題。
Proposition	論題	討論の対象となる意見。「〜だ」「〜すべきである」など断定文の型をとる。
Affirmative Speech (AS)	肯定側立論	肯定側チームが、論題を支持する主な理由を論証して説明すること。
Affirmative Team (AT)	肯定側チーム	論題を支持する立場を取るチーム
Negative Speech (NS)	否定側立論	否定側チームが、論題を支持しない主な理由を論証して説明すること。
Negative Team (NT)	否定側チーム	論題を支持しない立場を取るチーム
Cross Examination (CE)	質疑	相手チームの議論を明確にしたり、論証の不備をほのめかしたりすること。
Rebuttal	反駁（はんばく）	相手チームの議論に反論したり、根拠の優劣を比較したりすること。
Summary	要約	自分のチームの立場から議論を要約すること。立論や反駁の要点を含める。
Argument	議論	証拠や論拠に基づいた論議。
Position Statement	立場表明	論題に対する自らの立場を簡潔に主張すること。
Reason	根拠 / 理由	なぜ、その立場を取るのか説明すること。
Evidence	証拠	自らの主張や議論を支えるもので、事実、経験談、統計、事例、専門家の意見などがある。
Cite/Reference	引用する	証拠の情報源を明らかに示すこと。
Research	調査（する）	証拠資料を探すこと。
Source	証拠資料 / 情報源	自らの主張を裏付ける情報源。
Taking Notes (Flowing)	メモを取ること	ディベート中、論証や反駁の主要点を時系列的に正確に記録すること。
Judge	ジャッジ	論題に対して、肯定側・否定側のどちらの論が優れていたかを決めること。または試合を判定する審判。

References by Topic

Food

- Brown, J. (2018, November 28). *Is breakfast really the most important meal of the day?* BBC. http://www.bbc.com/future/story/20181126-is-breakfast-good-for-your-health

- Buckner, S. L., Loprinzi, P. D., & Loenneke, J. P. (2016). Why don't more people eat breakfast? A biological perspective. *The American Journal of Clinical Nutrition*, 103(6), 1555–1556. https://doi.org/10.3945/ajcn.116.132837

- Cahill, L. E., Chiuve, S. E., & Mekary, R. A. (2014). Prospective study of breakfast eating and incident coronary heart disease in a cohort of male US health professionals [Abstract]. *Journal of Vascular Surgery*, 59(2), 555. https://doi.org/10.1016/j.jvs.2013.12.009

- Chang-Claude, J., Hermann, S., Eilber, U., & Steindorf, K. (2005). Lifestyle determinants and mortality in German vegetarians and health-conscious persons: Results of a 21-year follow-up. *Cancer Epidemiology Biomarkers & Prevention*, 14(4), 963–968. https://doi.org/10.1158/1055-9965.epi-04-0696

- Craig, W. J., & Mangels, A. R. (2009). Position of the American Dietetic Association: vegetarian Diets [Abstract]. *Journal of the American dietetic association*, 109(7), 1266.

- Fraser, G. E., & Shavlik, D. J. (2001). Ten years of life: Is it a matter of choice? *Archives of Internal Medicine*, 161(13), 1645. https://doi.org/10.1001/archinte.161.13.1645

- Gallagher, J. (2016, January 4). *Diet debate: Is breakfast a waste of time?* BBC. https://www.bbc.com/news/health-35150598

- Herrmann, W., Schorr, H., Obeid, R., & Geisel, J. (2003). Vitamin B-12 status, particularly holotranscobalamin II and methylmalonic acid concentrations, and hyperhomocysteinemia in vegetarians. *The American Journal of Clinical Nutrition*, 78(1), 131–136. https://doi.org/10.1093/ajcn/78.1.131

- Hutchison, C. (2010, September 29). *Nutritionist does Twinkie and steak diet, loses weight.* ABC News. https://abcnews.go.com/Health/Recipes/twinkie-diet-short-term-fix-long-term-problem/story?id=11756710

- Kahleova, H., Lloren, J. I., Mashchak, A., Hill, M., & Fraser, G. E. (2017). Meal frequency and timing are associated with changes in body mass index in adventist health study 2. *The Journal of Nutrition*, 147(9), 1722–1728. https://doi.org/10.3945/jn.116.244749

- Key, T. J., Fraser, G. E., Thorogood, M., Appleby, P. N., Beral, V., Reeves, G., Burr, M. L., Chang-Claude, J., Frentzel-Beyme, R., Kuzma, J. W., Mann, J., & McPherson, K. (1999). Mortality in vegetarians and nonvegetarians: Detailed findings from a collaborative analysis of 5 prospective studies. *The American Journal of Clinical Nutrition*, 70(3), 516s-524s. https://doi.org/10.1093/ajcn/70.3.516s

- Leidy, H. J., Gwin, J. A., Roenfeldt, C. A., Zino, A. Z., & Shafer, R. S. (2016). Evaluating the intervention-based evidence surrounding the causal role of breakfast on markers of weight management, with specific focus on breakfast composition and size. *Advances in Nutrition*, 7(3), 563S-575S. https://doi.org/10.3945/an.115.010223
- Littlecott, H. J., Moore, G. F., Moore, L., Lyons, R. A., & Murphy, S. (2015). Association between breakfast consumption and educational outcomes in 9-11-year-old children. *Public Health Nutrition*, 19(9), 1583–1583. https://doi.org/10.1017/s1368980015003365
- Loth, S. (2018, June 19). Revealed: T*he cereals with more added sugar than biscuits – which?* News. Which? https://www.which.co.uk/news/2018/06/revealed-the-cereals-with-more-added-sugar-than-biscuits/
- Shibata, H., Nagai, H., Haga, H., Yasumura, S., Suzuki, T., & Suyama, Y. (1992). Nutrition for the Japanese elderly. *Nutrition and Health*, 8(2-3), 165-175.
- Tong, T. Y., Appleby, P. N., Bradbury, K. E., Perez-Cornago, A., Travis, R. C., Clarke, R., & Key, T. J. (2019). Risks of ischaemic heart disease and stroke in meat eaters, fish eaters, and vegetarians over 18 years of follow-up: results from the prospective EPIC-Oxford study. *BMJ*, 366, Article l4897.
- World Cancer Research Fund, & American Institute for Cancer Research. (2007). *Food, nutrition, physical activity, and the prevention of cancer: A global perspective*.

Environment

- *Booking.com reveals key findings from its 2019 sustainable travel report*. (2019, April 17). Booking.com. https://globalnews.booking.com/bookingcom-reveals-key-findings-from-its-2019-sustainable-travel-report/
- Butler, A. (2018, November 21). Do customers really care about your environmental impact? *Forbes*. https://www.forbes.com/sites/forbesnycouncil/2018/11/21/do-customers-really-care-about-your-environmental-impact/#5a02c8b6240d
- Is Japan eco-friendly or eco-hostile? (2017, August 29). *Nikkei Asian Review*. https://asia.nikkei.com/Business/Is-Japan-eco-friendly-or-eco-hostile
- Kommenda, N. (2019, July 19). How your flight emits as much CO_2 as many people do in a year. *The Guardian*. https://www.theguardian.com/environment/ng-interactive/2019/jul/19/carbon-calculator-how-taking-one-flight-emits-as-much-as-many-people-do-in-a-year
- *Plastic bags usage at Japanese stores down by 50%, but plastic bags sales through the roof*. (2020, August 16). Japan Today. https://japantoday.com/category/business/plastic-bag-usage-at-japanese-stores-down-by-50-but-plastic-bags-sales-through-the-roof

Technology

- Baker, P. C. (2019, October 3). Collision course: Why are cars killing more and more pedestrians? *The Guardian.*

  https://www.theguardian.com/technology/2019/oct/03/collision-course-pedestrian-deaths-rising-driverless-cars

- Bocas, J. (2018). *5 emerging technologies that will change healthcare.* Chief Healthcare Executive.
  https://www.idigitalhealth.com/news/5-emerging-technologies-that-will-change-healthcare

- *Fatal accidents by elderly drivers in Japan up 10 pct in 2018.* (2019, February 14). Nippon.com.
  https://www.nippon.com/en/news/yjj2019021400644/fatal-accidents-by-elderly-drivers-in-japan-up-10-pct-in-2018.html

- Japan convenience stores plan next generation of self-checkout. (2017, April 17). *Nikkei Asian Review.*
  https://asia.nikkei.com/Business/Japan-convenience-stores-plan-next-generation-of-self-checkout

- Statista Research Development. (2021, March 16). *Industrial robots: Statistics and facts.* Statista.
  https://www.statista.com/topics/1476/industrial-robots/

- Utermohlen, K. (2018, April 13). *15 artificial intelligence (AI) stats you need to know in 2018.* Towards Data Science.
  https://towardsdatascience.com/15-artificial-intelligence-ai-stats-you-need-to-know-in-2018-b6c5eac958e5

- Aoki, E. (2022, November 26). Danger-detecting AI system tested at Japan kindergarten. *The Mainichi.*
  https://mainichi.jp/english/articles/20221126/p2a/00m/0na/015000c

- Creighton, J. (2022, November 30). *The unavoidable problem of self-improvement in AI: An Interview with Ramana Kumar, part 1.* Future of Life Institute.
  https://futureoflife.org/recent-news/the-unavoidable-problem-of-self-improvement-in-ai-an-interview-with-ramana-kumar-part-1/

- Digital News Group. (2023, May 23). Most people in Japan want to use AI at work but worried it "will take away jobs": Poll. *The Mainichi.* https://mainichi.jp/english/articles/20230523/p2a/00m/0na/006000c

- Meah, J. (2023, June 5). *Ai in Cybersecurity: The future of hacking is here.* Techopedia.
  https://www.techopedia.com/ai-in-cybersecurity-the-future-of-hacking-is-here/2/34520

Media

- Emmons, S. (2013). Is media violence damaging to kids? CNN.
  https://edition.cnn.com/2013/02/21/living/parenting-kids-violence-media/index.html

- Riehm, K. E., Feder, K. A., Tormohlen, K. N., Crum, R. M., Young, A. S., Green, K. M., Pacek, L. R., La Flair, L. N., & Mojtabai, R. (2019). Associations between time spent using social media and internalizing and externalizing problems among US youth. *JAMA Psychiatry*, 76(12), 1266-1273. https://doi.org/10.1001/jamapsychiatry.2019.2325

- Strauss, M. (2014, July). *Celebrity influence on kids' body image.* Novak Djokovic Foundation.

https://novakdjokovicfoundation.org/celebrity-influence-on-kids-body-image/
- Tankovska, H. (2021, January 28). *Number of global social network users 2017-2025.* Statista.

  https://www.statista.com/statistics/278414/number-of-worldwide-social-network-users/

Gender
- Aizawa, Y. (2018, December 21). *Gender equality in Japan remains bottom.* NHK WORLD-JAPAN.

  https://www3.nhk.or.jp/nhkworld/en/news/backstories/335/
- Aley, M., & Hahn, L. (2020). The powerful male hero: A content analysis of gender representation in posters for children's animated movies. *Sex Roles*, 83, 499-509.

  http://doi:10.1007/s11199-020-01127-z
- Knorr, C. (2017). *What media teach kids about gender can have lasting effects, report says.* CNN.

  https://edition.cnn.com/2017/06/29/health/gender-stereotypes-media-children-partner/index.html
- Schneider. M. (2018). *New dads don't want to take paternity leave. Here's why you should encourage them.* Inc.

  https://www.inc.com/michael-schneider/new-dads-dont-want-to-take-paternity-leave-heres-why-you-should-encourage-them.html
- Yamaguchi, K. (2019). Japan's gender gap: A lack of gender equality in career opportunity and long work hours perpetuate wage differences between men and women. *Finance and Development*, 56(1), 26-29.

  https://www.imf.org/external/pubs/ft/fandd/2019/03/pdf/gender-equality-in-japan-yamaguchi.pdf
- Ministry of Foreign Affairs of Japan (2022, December 5). World assembly for women: WAW! 2022 concept note: Gender wage gap. https://www.mofa.go.jp/fp/hr_ha/page22e_001005.html

Discussion Skills Review
- Fearn-Wannan, J., Kita, S., Sturges, J. G., & Young, D. (2020). *What's your opinion? Interactive skills for effective discussion: Book II* (1st ed.). DTP Publishing.

Sample Debate
- Fraga, J. (2019, February 25). *Here's how living in a city can mess with your mental health.* Healthline.

  https://www.healthline.com/health/mental-health/living-in-a-city
- Jojo Kigyo Search (2021). *Nihon no Kakutodouhuken no Kabushikigaisha-su to Jojokaisha-su* [Companies and publicly listed companies in each prefecture in Japan].

  https://xn--vckya7nx51ik9ay55a3l3a.com/analyses/number_of_companies
- LIFULL HOME'S. (2020, September 14). *Daigakusei no Hitorigurashi Yachin 6 manen wa Takai? Shiokuri kara Seikatsushi Gakuseimuke Bukken no Sagashikata made Shokai* [University students living alone. Is 60,000 yen too expensive? Information about remittance, living cost, and apartments for students.] https://www.homes.co.jp/cont/rent/rent_00639/
- Ministry of Health, Labor, and Welfare. (n.d.). *Chiikibetsu Saitei Chingin no Zenkoku Ichiran* [The minimum wage in all prefectures in Japan].

https://www.mhlw.go.jp/stf/seisakunitsuite/bunya/ koyou_roudou/roudoukijun/minimumichiran/

- Nuwer, R. (2018, June 1). *Is it really healthier to live in the countryside?* BBC. https://www.bbc.com/future/article/20180531-where-are-the-worlds-healthiest-places-to-live

- Pflum, M. (2019, July 13). *Cities to see more job growth in coming decades, rural areas not so much, study says.* NBC News.
  https://www.nbcnews.com/business/economy/cities-see-more-job-growth-coming-decades-rural-areas-not-n1029481

- Shuyo 126sha Anketo: Korona-go mo Zaitaku Kigyo 9 wari Kuni Kankyoseibi Kyumu ni [Survey for 126 major companies: 90% after COVID-19 ends. The government needs to prepare working environments]. (2021, January 30). *Mainichi Shimbun*. https://mainichi.jp/articles/20210130/ddm/003/020/145000c

- Statistics Japan. (2020.) *Convenience stores*. ODOMON. https://stats-japan.com/t/kiji/10328

memo

memo

本書には CD（別売）があります

Debate to Go
Essential Methods and Practice for Debating and Discussion
大学生のためのディベート基本演習

2024 年 1 月 30 日 初版第 1 刷発行
2024 年 2 月 20 日 初版第 2 刷発行

編　者	三　島　雅　一
	Jamie G. Sturges
著　者	学校法人立教学院 立教大学外国語教育研究センター
発行者	福　岡　正　人
発行所	株式会社 **金 星 堂**

（〒101-0051）東京都千代田区神田神保町 3-21
Tel.（03）3263-3828（営業部）
　　（03）3263-3997（編集部）
Fax（03）3263-0716
https://www.kinsei-do.co.jp

編集担当／長島吉成　　　　　　　　　　　　Printed in Japan
印刷所・製本所／加藤文明社

ISBN978-4-7647-4204-8　　　C1082

Feedback Form
&
Worksheets
(for submission)

Debate Reflection Form (Mid-term Debate)

● Things which your team could do better

● Things which you learned from the other team

● How you contributed to preparing for the debate

● What you could do better for a debate next time

Name: _____

Date: _____

Debate Reaction Form (Mid-term Debate)

● Your proposition:

● Explain the arguments made by both teams.

● Which team did better or was more convincing? Why?

Name: _____

Date: _____

Debate Reflection Form (Final Debate)

● Things which your team could do better

● Things which you learned from the other team

● How you contributed to preparing for the debate

● What you could do better for a debate next time

Name: _____

Date: _____

.

Debate Reaction Form (Final Debate)

● Your proposition:

● Explain the arguments made by both teams.

● Which team did better or was more convincing? Why?

Name: _____

Date: _____

Lesson 1: Worksheet

What is Debate? (p.4)

Do you know what a debate is? Use this worksheet to make a list of things you know about debate. Cut out the worksheet and submit it to the instructor at the end of the lesson.

Name: _____

Date: _____

Lesson 4: Worksheet

Practice (p.22)

Use this worksheet to write your argument. Remember to include all the necessary parts of an argument. Cut out the worksheet and submit it to the instructor at the end of the lesson.

Name: _____

Date: _____

Lesson 6: Worksheet

Practice (p.32)

Use this worksheet to write a summary of the debate for the Affirmative Team. Remember the points from "What is summary?" and use the phrases from Useful Expressions for Making Summaries to help you. Cut out the worksheet and submit it to the instructor at the end of the lesson.

Name: _____

Date: _____

Lesson 12: Worksheet

Practice (p.55)

Use this worksheet to write a summary. Use Useful Expressions for Making Summaries on Page 31. Include phrases from the Overall Summary, Focused Summary, and Connecting Your Summary to the Proposition. Cut out the worksheet and submit it to the instructor at the end of the lesson.

Name: _____

Date: _____